What's In It For Me?

◆

How a Self-Centered Bad Boy,
Became a God-Centered
Businessman

◆

JOSEPH M. WARREN

"The meaning of life is to find your gift.
The purpose of life is to give it away."
~ **Pablo Picasso**

Produced by:
Tara Richter - www.RichterPublishing.com

Edited by:
Casey Cavanagh, Brittany Graves, & Miki West

Book Cover Designed by:
Andrew "AJ" Favicchio - www.SauceOnTap.com

Cover Photograph by:
Barry Lively - www.LivelyNow.com

Copyright © 2014 Joseph M. Warren

ISBN-10:0615991467
ISBN-13:9780615991467

To find out more about
Joseph Warren, any of his
products or services, or if you'd
like to hire him to speak at your
next event, please visit:
www.JosephWarren.net

DISCLAIMER

This book is designed to provide information on entrepreneurship only. This information is provided and sold with the knowledge that the publisher and author do not offer any legal or medical advice. In the case of a need for any such expertise consult with the appropriate professional. This book does not contain all information available on the subject. This book has not been created to be specific to any individual people or organizations' situation or needs. Reasonable efforts have been made to make this book as accurate as possible. However, there may be typographical and or content errors. Therefore, this book should serve only as a general guide and not as the ultimate source of subject information. This book contains information that might be dated or erroneous and is intended only to educate and entertain. The author and publisher shall have no liability or responsibility to any person or entity regarding any loss or damage incurred, or alleged to have incurred, directly or indirectly, by the information contained in this book or as a result of anyone acting or failing to act upon the information in this book. You hereby agree never to sue and to hold the author and publisher harmless from any and all claims arising out of the information contained in this book. You hereby agree to be bound by this disclaimer, covenant not to sue and release. You may return this book within the guarantee time period for a full refund. In the interest of full disclosure, this book contains affiliate links that might pay the author or publisher a commission upon any purchase from the company. While the author and publisher take no responsibility for any virus or technical issues that could be caused by such kinks, the business practices of these companies and or the performance of any product or service, the author or publisher has used the product or service and makes a recommendation in good faith based on that experience.

All characters appearing in this work are fictitious. Any resemblance to real persons, living or dead is purely coincidental.

DEDICATION

Edward M. Kobel, President & COO of DeBartolo Development in Tampa, FL. Thank you for introducing me to the concept of "Marketplace Ministry" and inviting me into your men's leadership group. This was the beginning of my transformation journey. Your example has shown me how a business leader can be God-centered and still be incredibly successful in the marketplace.

John Farris, Pastor of Cross Pointe Church in Clearwater, Florida. Thank you for guiding me through the confusion of letting go of my old lifestyle and moving towards a more God-centered way of living.

Tom Wolf, Author of *Identity & Destiny™*. Thank you for leading me through your powerful program. Through it I learned to "hear" the quiet whisper of the Lord and for this I am eternally grateful to you.

Gentlemen, without the three of you I wouldn't be where I am today, nor would I be able to share my story from darkness to light. Through you, God entered my broken world and changed everything.

JOSEPH M. WARREN

CONTENTS

PASSION # 3: FAITH

ACKNOWLEDGMENTS

*I would like to thank and acknowledge
all the people who made this book possible:*

Heather Young Kendell - Thank you for your awesome friendship, I have learned so much from you. I appreciate your tireless service to everyone at CoCreativ.

Jason Stoll – Thank you for your friendship, your undying loyalty, and your steadfast belief in God's vision for CoCreativ.

Andrew Favicchio - Thank you for your great videography and design work. Your talents are unmatched.

Tara Richter (Richter Publishing) - Thank you for simplifying the entire writing and publishing process for me. I could not have created this book without you.

My Family - Thank you all for helping to shape me into the man that I've become. We have struggled through much together but God holds our future and will not leave us orphans. I believe in each of you and love you immensely.

JOSEPH M. WARREN

INTRODUCTION

**I used to be an immature self-centered boy.
Now I'm a successful God-centered businessman.**

Here's my story.

How does someone become successful in business and life, without becoming someone they're not?

Today's society says it's not cool to be religious. We're told to keep "church and state" separate, so that we don't offend anyone. *"Keep God out of business!"* But are you staying true to yourself and your beliefs when you keep your Faith bottled up inside?

My life is awesome now because in the past 12 months, I have discovered how to seamlessly combine my three passions ----- *Entrepreneurship, Self-Improvement, and Faith.*

However, it wasn't always this way. I did some crazy stuff along the way that almost killed me. I indulged in many sexual temptations to cover up deep wounds from my childhood.

I'm not perfect and it took me a third of my life, but I finally discovered how to make myself 100% complete --- 100% undivided --- one hundred percent Joseph. If you like, I can show you how.

Walk with me as I share with you my unbelievable transformation and how I was able to move my SELF out of the way and allow God to lead me to my "higher calling."

Here's part of my secret formula: Once you quiet all the outside noise of the world in your mind, you can finally hear the *Quiet Whisper of the Lord.*

Through His whisper, He'll reveal your Identity, your Destiny, and the specific Assignment(s) He wants you to carry out in the world.

No longer will you question, *"Why am I here? What is my purpose? What am I meant to do? Does God really have a plan for my life?"*

God has a perfect plan for your life that only you can achieve ----- no one else, just you.

When you see it, your life will never look the same.

You will have perfect clarity and that's when amazing things start to happen. That's when your life starts to have meaning and purpose. That's when God uses your life to set the world on fire!

Here's your opportunity to turn your life inside-out.

Are you ready?!

PASSION # 1

Entrepreneurship

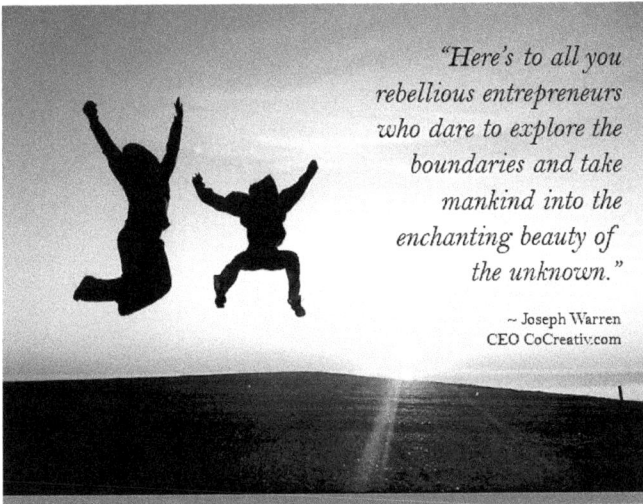

"Here's to all you rebellious entrepreneurs who dare to explore the boundaries and take mankind into the enchanting beauty of the unknown."

~ Joseph Warren
CEO CoCreativ.com

JOSEPH M. WARREN

CHAPTER 1

Conquering This One Thing Changed My Life Forever!

The most difficult thing to conquer in your business or your personal life is ----- yourself.

Unfortunately, like every great lesson, I had to learn this one the hard way...

I was scheduled to pitch investors for outside capital to grow one of my startup companies.

As CEO (the "face of the company"), I'm often responsible for pitching the deals.

We were scheduled to meet with a husband and wife investor team and it took two weeks to get this meeting set up. I was super excited that morning even though it had been a rough one. It was one of those mornings where everything went wrong. It began with my alarm NOT going off which set me way behind.

After getting showered and eating breakfast, I finally hit the road. Generally, I'd pre-drive the route to avoid any surprises. But I hadn't so now I was at the mercy of the unknown.

Sure enough, I ran into bumper-to-bumper construction. Ugh! Construction hazards were everywhere! I kept checking my watch and honking the horn. That's when the New-York-take-charge-driver in me came out and I started thinking *"I know I can find another way."* I hit the gas and cut down side streets to find a quicker route.

Amazingly, I managed to arrive three minutes early. As I walked into the office, I took a deeeeep breath to gain my composure.

I introduced myself to the woman at the front desk

who replied, *"I'm sorry but he is not here yet. He should be here in any minute."*

I now had a few minutes to gather myself since I was sort of frazzled trying to get there on time.

So I wait. Fifteen minutes go by. The husband still hasn't shown up. I went from feeling humble (like I needed to apologize to HIM), to instead feeling agitated (as though he needed to apologize to ME). Within that short window of time, my ego had inflated.

Finally, he walks in with his wife. She was as sweet as she can be. I introduce myself to him and extend my hand, "Good morning, I'm Joseph Warren, how are you?" He nods his head and says, *"Yeah,"* and walks right past me with his eyes plastered to his phone.

Right away this strikes me as rude. Just plain rude. I follow him to the conference room where he sits down and says very matter-of-factly, *"You can start now."*

Without a pause, I start my pitch. As I'm speaking, I notice that his wife and their two colleagues are paying close attention to me.

The only one who's not paying attention is him.

Instead, he's texting on his phone, just typing away with his little fingers. Ugh!

I started telling myself, *"Just let it go."* But then I'm thinking, *"Are you kidding me? I waited forever for him to start this meeting and now that we're all here, he's not even paying attention to me!?"*

He continued to text, but still I refrained from saying anything to him. Not only is he texting as I'm pitching, but he's not giving me any eye contact or anything.

Then his phone rings. He takes the call and walks out of the room. After a few minutes, I turn to his wife and ask, *"Is he coming back in?"*

She says, *"Oh please, just continue without him."*

"He's part of the decision, right?" I ask.

And she's replies with a noncommittal, *"Yeah."*

So, I say, *"I'd rather wait then, if that's okay. Could you possibly go see how he's doing?"*

She steps out into the hallway and I can hear them conversing. She says, *"He's waiting for you, he's waiting..."* and he replies, *"I'll be right there."*

Finally, he strolls back in and sits down. Still, he's

on his phone, texting away. I regain my composure and continue even though my ego is starting to hit the roof! He continued to ignore my presentation.

Finally, I hit my threshold of intolerance.

I just couldn't take it anymore and lashed out, *"You know what? We don't have to do this today. We spent two weeks scheduling this meeting and it's important to our company. We took time out of our schedule and we could be with other people right now, if you like. It's obvious that this isn't important to you."*

Shocked, he looks at his wife completely perplexed, *"What did I do? What did I do wrong?"*

I was dumbfounded, *"What did you do wrong? Dude, you're texting the entire time I'm talking, and frankly, that's just rude!"*

Desperately he replies, *"I'm not texting."* Then he holds his phone up and says, *"Look, I've been writing down everything you've been saying."*

"Gulp!" ----- Followed by awkward silence.

Ugh! I felt so embarrassed. I had let my ego take over and lost control. I knew the meeting was over right then and there.

I completely ruined it for my team because I assumed he wasn't paying attention to me.

My big fat ego killed the deal.

PRINCIPLE #1:

Be patient and don't assume anything about a person's intentions. You probably don't have all the facts.

You don't know where other people are coming from. You don't know what's going on in their lives. You don't know what they're thinking. You don't know what they've been through. There is so much about them that you just don't know.

Don't assume because 9 out of 10 times people are coming from a good place. We've been so jaded by the media that we think people are trying to do us wrong. That's a lie. It's self-sabotage.

I assumed the investor was texting when he was actually taking notes. I was wrong. The worst part was driving home with my cofounders in silence, knowing that I obliterating this great opportunity for all of us. I failed my team. Moral of the story: *Big egos equal big disasters.*

Sometimes, you find yourself in the middle of nowhere; and sometimes, in the middle of nowhere, you find yourself

CHAPTER 2

I Became Unstoppable With This Simple Yet Powerful 30-Second Trick!

At 19 years old, I started a professional fundraising company that specialized in raising funds for large non-profit organizations such as The National Center for Missing & Exploited Children (NCMEC).

PAIN: Many charities are not very good at raising money for the causes they represent.

<u>SOLUTION</u>: We went out every day and raised money for these organizations so they could continue supporting their great causes.
In layman's terms, we were the small "for profit" that raised money for the large non-profits.

We did all the hard grunt work and handed them, pretty much, "free" money while taking a transactional fee for our services.

I had a team of 50 people on the streets, raising money every single day. It was a really interesting model that we were exploring back then.

Our first location was in Chicago. Within 12 months, we raised $2,000,000 for charities. It was somewhat amazing what we were building.

Frank was my Assistant Manager at the time. He was one of those insanely "wired" high-energy individuals. And he looked the part too.

He resembled a WWF wrestler-----a mix of Hulk Hogan and Randy "Macho Man" Savage. He had the long, jagged, straight bleach-blonde hair and would literally jump out in front of people in parking lots and ask them for money.

Many thought he was crazy but, but they would still hand over their hard-earned cash to him. **He was good at what he did.**

Out of 50 people in my company, Frank was my number one guy so when we wanted to expand to the West Coast, we sent Frank out there first.

Soon after he arrived, he immediately ran into total, complete, and absolute failure. Yes, absolute failure.

Frank was a high-energy guy who was unstoppable in Chicago, but when he hit Los Angeles he was stopped-in-his-tracks by massive and consistent rejection. I felt like he was losing his fundraising "mojo."

He would call me on the phone all depressed, *"Joseph, it's so different out here. It's not like Chicago. Chicago is easy man. Out here, people are nasty! I mean they're straight up rude. They're cussing me out in every which way. I start to talk, but before I get the words out, they threaten to call the cops. It's harsh bro."*

Week after week, he would complain.

Mostly, I would just listen to him.

See I was wired different than Frank. Back then, I had this confidence about me where I wouldn't ever take 'NO' for an answer on anything. My presentation style wasn't as intense as Frank's was but somehow, I always got what I wanted.

I started thinking, *"Hmmm. Maybe he's lost it. Maybe he's lost that drive, because I know I can go out there right now and crush it. He probably just hasn't figured out how to do it yet."*

This went on for about a month.

I thought he would eventually turn it around on his own, but he didn't. His numbers were just pathetic from what we were getting back in the reports, and I could hear in his voice that he was ready to quit after all the nasty rejection.

Finally, I had enough of his whining and said, *"You know what Frank? I'm going to come out there and help you get LA started."*

He sounded so relieved.

The day I arrived in Los Angeles, I became Frank's roommate and moved into his tiny 10'x10' room in some crack motel in Inglewood, CA. It was straight up disgusting. Every night, our prostitute neighbors would knock on our door to see if we wanted to "party". No thanks.

My second day there, we went out together so I could see and experience what he had been telling me over the phone. We got up bright and early, drove to a random location, and started walking door-to-door, business-to-business.

People call this soliciting. That's what we did, and we were fearless at it.

When people said, *"No soliciting!"* we'd just pitch right through it, as if they were excited to see us. After a while, we couldn't even hear it anymore and that only emboldened our confidence.

We pulled up to a strip mall with about 10 stores.

As Frank opened the first door, (before we even walked inside the place) we heard someone shouting at the top of their lungs, *"GET THE 'F' OUT OF HERE, YOU SONS OF B-TCHES!*

*YOU MOTHER F-ERS! I'M CALLING THE COPS!
LEAVE! GO!"*

<u>I was shocked!</u> Frank immediately closed the door.
Startled, I asked him, *"What the heck was that?"*

Sarcastically he replied, *"Welcome to Los Angeles.
This is what I've been telling you about, Joseph."*

So we went to the next store, and again, *"GET THE
'F' OUT OF HERE, YOU SONS OF B-TCHES! YOU
MOTHER F-ERS! I'M CALLING THE COPS!"*

After several stores I realized this wasn't a "Frank"
issue. This was a *new territory* issue. We never
even got to say what we were doing because they
wouldn't let us get a word out. They just kept
SCREAMING very abusive language at us.

It was normal for us to carry a handful of cash to
show that others were donating to the cause.
Combine that with all our credentials and we
should immediately look legit.

But here, we were nothing more than "Solicitors".
Scum of the earth. Non-humans.

It happened the same way every time we went into a business. We got the same abusive reaction.

We walked into 10 businesses back-to-back. We left all 10 with insults, threats and no pitch. We had zero donations. This was not looking good.

I suggested we take an early lunch break (I really just needed a moment to figure out what the heck was going on).

As we sat down for lunch, Frank says to me, *"I told you. It's sick, it's crazy man. Let's just pack up and go back to Chicago. Please, please, please. I'm so done with it here."*

To me it was obvious that we were missing something, and it was obvious that we were not connecting with these people even though they were no different than our typical target audience back in Chicago.

Then I realized something.

What we were doing in Chicago worked in Chicago, but it didn't work in Los Angeles.

There has to be a lesson here: _What works in one place, doesn't always work in the other._ Or, what works in one business, may not work in another business. So, what were we missing?

As I ate my last bite, it hit me, _"Frank I have an idea!"_ He looked in my eyes and saw that all too familiar spark of creative-brilliance.

For the first time in a month, Frank smiled.

We went onto the next business. It was a jewelry shop, (the kind where they buzz people in) making our approach even more difficult.

I turned to Frank and said, _"Here's what I want you to do. I want you to follow my lead. I'm going to walk in very fast. I want you to keep at my heels. Keep up with me. All I want you to do is stare with intense confidence, like you're pissed off. Can you do that?"_

He looked confused, _"Yeah, but why?"_ I replied, _"Don't worry about it. Just do it."_ He agreed.

I put my credentials behind my back and had Frank do the same.

When we reached the door, I waved with a big smile and they buzzed us in probably thinking we were potential customers. After I heard the "buzz", I threw open the door, let my credentials out from behind my back, and walked full speed ahead with Frank nipping at my heels.

Immediately, the guy behind the counter starts shouting at us, *"GET THE 'F' OUT YOU SONS OF B-TCHES...I'M CALLING THE COPS!"*

Frank is stuck to me like glue, walking full speed.

I locked eyes with the guy yelling and shouted back, *"SHUT UP AND SIT DOWN!"*

The whole place went dead quiet (remember, this is a jewelry store, so the customers probably thought they were being robbed).

I remember thinking to myself, *"Just follow through. Just follow through."*

The owner, although startled, paused for a few seconds then shouts again, *"I SAID GET OUT OF HERE! I'M CALLING THE COPS! ARE YOU F-ING STUPID OR SOMETHING?!"*

I shouted back even louder, practically climbing over the glass case, *"I SAID SHUT UP AND SIT DOWN!"*

The guy's butt hit his seat at 100 mph and everybody was frozen solid.

I could see Frank behind me in a quiet, nervous panic, trying his best to support what I'm doing but he didn't have a clue what's going on.

I lowered my voice and continued, *"Listen, we're not here for anything other than a really great cause. We're helping kids. I'm not soliciting. We're helping children. Now, here's what we're going to do. You and I are going to bring our volume down, and we're going to talk to each other like human beings. We're not going to yell at each other. We're going to treat each other with respect, and we're not going to yell any more. You're going to hear me out. I don't care if you help or not but you will listen to me. You will give me that respect. Agreed?"*

Confused and somewhat scared, he agreed.

I did my 30 second pitch (but now it's emboldened with insane confidence because I just controlled another human being and made him subject to me). I already knew I was getting money from him. I continued, *"Plus it's a tax write off, 100% legit, and you can check us out."*

In a normal tone the owner replied, *"Listen, I appreciate you guys but all over the news, they're telling people not to donate to ANY charities because 99% of them are scams, so how do I know you're legit? I have no problem helping, especially for kids, but how do I know?"*

[I later learned that there were more than 6,000 charities in Los Angeles alone and yes, 99 percent of them were scams. Aha! The real problem was now revealed. We must prove our credibility.]

Mini lesson: If you listen well, customers will always tell you the real problem they have with you, your product, or your service.

I showed him our credentials and gave him our phone numbers and told him to call anyone he wanted.

But he still needed reassurance so I said, *"We are 100% legit and the bottom line is this, I get that*

there's a lot of scams out there, but not donating to anyone is hurting the few good ones. So what's going to happen? The legit ones won't be able to help all those kids just because the media is scaring you. Is that really what you want to happen?"
He seemed satisfied with my logic and asked how much we wanted.

"$10 plus it's 100% tax deductible, and we even give you a nice thank you gift for supporting the cause."

He hands me $10 and I write him a receipt. Then I turn to his customers who all just happened to be pulling out ten dollar bills, too. I took their money and wrote them each a receipt. BOOM!

But before leaving I told the owner, *"We're going to come back once a week. You're going to donate $10 every week and we're going to give you a tax deductible receipt for your donation."*

Surprisingly, he agreed.

As soon as we walked out and around the corner, Frank could barely contain himself and blurts out, *"WHAT THE HECK WAS THAT!?"*

With bold confidence I looked him in the eyes and said, *"Frank... THAT is how we're going to take over Los Angeles."*

Later that day, we literally hit 30 businesses in a row and <u>everyone</u> donated even though they had cursed us out a few minutes earlier.

Within 12 months, we raised just under $2 million dollars in one of the worst fundraising cities in America.

PRINCIPLE #2:

What works in one place, doesn't always work in another.

Always be ready for change. Whether good or bad, nothing stays the same. To be successful in the world of business, you must be a problem solver. You must be resilient.

When something's not working, you can complain and quit, or find out why it's not working.

Success is always a decision. So is failure.

PRINCIPLE #3:

Always "mirror" the person you're speaking with. Then add 10% more.

Literally become a mirror image of others. If they treat you aggressively, give them the same back (but do it 10% more) so they become subject to you, and not the other way around. When they treat you nice and with respect, do the same back but give them 10% more.

Don't change who you are. If you're a loving person, don't become an unloving person just because someone's verbally bashing you.

Sometimes, you'll need to help people recognize your self-worth in the moment. You can do this by abruptly taking control of the conversation.

Instantly, you'll have their respect ----- if you <u>claim</u> it. You must claim it. Sometimes, you have to claim what you want in life.

When two people meet for the first time, whoever is more certain will always influence the other.

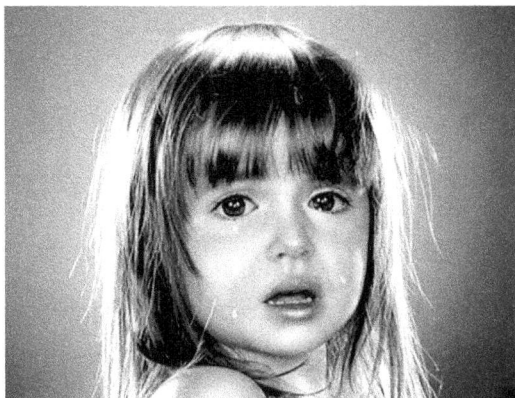

CHAPTER 3

Deep Down I Was Crying Like A Scared Little Girl!

Less than a month had passed since we learned how to conquer LA. It was working. Frank and I started a hiring frenzy to build up our staff. We took people out on training days so they could see exactly what we did and find out if they could too.

It was a pretty eye-opening experience for most applicants. Imagine going on a job interview where you tag along with us as we solicit door-to-door.

You watch us get yelled at and then watch us yell back until we take control of the situation. After each pitch, we walk out with money and respect.

Not your typical interview process, right?

There was something about that, though. There was some power in that. It attracted people and got them thinking, *"What the heck is this? I want to try. Can I try?"*

Maybe people have a lot of anger inside that they really want to get out. Maybe yelling at people for a good cause was exactly what they needed.

On one particular day, I picked a location but didn't know anything about the area. I had just picked it randomly on a map.

As I parked, all of a sudden, I felt a lot of tension coming from the three "trainees" who were in my car. They were all completely quiet and frozen stiff.

I turned to them and said, *"Okay guys, let's get going."* They stared at me with eyes full of terror.

They desperately explained that the area I picked for the day was none other than Compton, Los Angeles.

(I didn't know it at the time but Compton was featured in many gangster rap songs, noted for being one of the most dangerous cities in America.)

Immune to their fear, I persuaded them to get out of the car so we could get to work. As we started down the sidewalk, I noticed they were walking like three huddled mice, all close together on my heels.

I found their behavior peculiar but I just kept walking. I was completely "green behind the ears" regarding our situation. I had never heard of Compton before. To me, it's just another city. It's just another day of work and we were there to raise some money for kids. That's it.

We got about a block down the street from where we parked and all of a sudden we hear, *"BANG, BANG! BANG, BANG!"* Four gun shots.

I had never heard a real gun shot before so I asked, *"What the heck was that?"* I had this big naïve smile on my face.

No answer.

I turned around but my three trainees had mysteriously disappeared and were nowhere in sight. Why?

Can you believe that they were all face down on the sidewalk crying and whimpering like children?!

Still naive, I ask again what the noises were. They all start shouting, *"Gunshots! Get down!"*

I thought they were acting ridiculous. Finally, after some convincing, they get back up and start following me again, but not without relentless complaints and pleading to go home.

We continue walking to the 7-Eleven on the corner where we could see a police car and a crowd of people forming. Because there was a cop car, we were safe, right?

Wrong. It turns out that the gunshots we heard were aimed at a police officer who was coming out of the 7-Eleven. <u>Someone had gunned him down in cold blood.</u>

We were NOT safe there.

The trainees scampered into the 7-Eleven and kept begging me to take them home.

I finally said to the group, *"Listen, no offense, but I'm going to continue on. You guys do whatever you want to do. Call a taxi or something."*

So they did.

I was still in denial and decided to keep walking down the street. As I'm walking, I realized that the neighborhood was getting worse and worse. Literally, everything was boarded up and there wasn't a living soul in sight except for the occasional prostitutes standing on the corner.

Still I kept walking.

At the end of a street I could see a barbershop with an "OPEN" sign. I thought to myself, *"Yes, finally a business!"*

(Actually, it was just a *front* for drug dealers.)

As I walked up, I did my typical "throw the door open" approach. Sitting at the end of this long narrow "barbershop", there were six big black guys, all in black trench coats and gold chains.

My proven approach was to focus in on one person, so I zeroed in on the guy in the middle. Full-speed with my arm extended for a handshake, I walked at him.

He couldn't get away from me fast enough. He literally fell back off his chair just to avoid my hand. Immediately, they all reach into their jackets and grab their guns. Guns?! WTF?

I assume they didn't draw their guns because they thought I was a cop.

One of them nervously shouted, *"Yo man, waz up? What you want?"*

I replied with my normal 30 second pitch.

"No man, you a cop. You five-o!"

After some tense conversation back and forth, I finally convinced him I wasn't a cop, *"I'm just trying to raise money for kids."*

Immediately, he smiled, puffed out his chest and signaled for the six of them to surround me.

This guy who's been talking the whole time (obviously their leader), looks me in the eye and smirks, *"I have a better idea. Instead of us donating to you, how about you donate to us?"*

Then he looks down at the handful of cash in my hands.

Oooops.

It's taken some time, but I finally understood the dangerous situation I put myself in.

Sh#t!

I was about to get mugged by six really big black guys. They were roughly six-foot-three or four and easily 240lbs each. Some of them were even a little bigger than that and all of them were "packing" guns.

I now realized the severity of the situation and at this point, there was no getting out of it.

My life was now in jeopardy.

I took a small step back, squared up my legs and I braced myself for whatever was about to happen. Then something triggered in my head, and I remembered, something I read in a book once:

"Whenever you're outnumbered, identify the leader of the group. Once you know who the leader of the group is, you must intimidate him, more than he's intimidating you. If you do that successfully, you'll probably have a one percent chance of survival (as opposed to zero chance)."

Even a 1% chance of survival sounded good to me at this moment.

I took a deep breath, gained my composure and looked their *leader* in the eye.

Deep down I was crying like a scared little girl.

"Listen. You need to know one thing and one thing only. Whatever your boyz are about to do to me, I really don't care. All you need to know right now is that whatever happens here, I'M TAKING YOU DOWN WITH ME. I not worried about them but you need to worry about me. Are you ready to die?"

I locked my gaze on him and wouldn't flinch.

He looked back deep into my eyes. I knew he was sizing me up to see if I was really a threat or not.

It was the most awkward 30 seconds of my life!

Pin-drop-silence ----- I stared at him and he stared at me ----- our eyes locked.

Inside, I was crying like a little 13 year-old girl, but I didn't break my hold. I had to make it believable.

I had to take the fear I was feeling and sell it back to him. I had to make him feel threatened.

I had to sell fear. My life depended on it.

After deafening silence, he leaned back a little, cocked his head and said, *"We just playin man. Relax. We just playin."*

I stayed locked on him as he continued, *"Dude, chill. Chill, bro. We just playin."*

I snapped back, *"You're just playin?! You need to know, right now, that I'm not. I'm about to take you out bro, so you need to get your boyz to back off right now! Tell them to take their hands off their guns, and step away from me. That's the first thing."*

He signaled to them and they backed away, removing their hands from their guns.

Now I had a little breathing room but I was still locked in battle mode, visualizing in vivid detail what I was going to do to him.

I had seen it in a movie once. It was probably not going to work. Actually, there was a very, very high chance that it wasn't going to work, but I didn't care. I was going to do it anyway.

My dumb plan: One step to his right side, slide under his right arm and around his back. As his gun drew, I would use it to pop all five of his boyz and use him as a human shield. Dumb, right?

(Like any young man, I thought I was invincible.)

I remained locked on him. And he stayed locked on me. His boyz were now standing behind him.

The tension was so thick, you could cut it.

Then I said, *"The number two thing you're going to do is you're going to open your wallet, and you're going to give me $10 for these kids."*

He laughed in my face, *"Yeah, right. We're not doing that, man."*

I said, *"Listen, you're drug dealers, right? You sell drugs on the street that end up in kids' hands? You destroy kids' lives? I'm giving you a chance to help save their lives for once. Plus, you just threatened my life and I'm still ready to drop your sorry ass ----- 10 bucks now, bro!"*

Awkward silence followed. Then slowly he reached into his pocket, pulled out his wallet, and handed me $10.

Emboldened, I said, *"And now $10 from each of your boyz!"*

Five guys handed me $10 each. I reached into my bag where I had a bunch of t-shirts that I used as "thank you" gifts for donating. I crumpled a shirt into a ball and threw it at him, *"Here's your freaking t-shirt bro!"*

His physiology instantly shifted a little bit and he glared back at me and said, *"You should leave now."*

Slowly I backed out facing him... all the way down this long narrow barbershop. I hit the glass door behind me and then backed out the rest of the way.

I ran to the corner, took a breath, and headed back to my car.

Later I thought to myself, *"If I can talk myself out of that situation, I can talk myself out of anything."*

In that moment, a huge burst of confidence came over me as well as a very healthy respect for being more cautious and less cocky.

PRINCIPLE #4:

When you are out-numbered (or out-gunned), make sure that your confidence trumps that of your opponent.

If you make a mistake and find yourself in a very poor or dangerous situation like I did, make sure that your confidence supersedes that of those around you, and 'talk' yourself out of it.

It's the same for business.

When you're pitching investors for outside funding, sometimes they can be aggressive and team up against you (almost like thugs with guns).

The situation may look different but the feeling of intimidation is the same. Literally, you need to be more confident than your opponent. By doing so, you will win over your enemy.

The trick with the guy in the barbershop was to get him to no longer think about what he was going to do to me, but instead to think about what I was going to do to him.

The moment I had him thinking about his own survival, I controlled the situation.

PASSION # 2

Self-Improvement

WE CANNOT
BECOME
WHAT WE
WANT
BY REMAINING
WHAT WE ARE.
-MAX DEPREE

JOSEPH M. WARREN

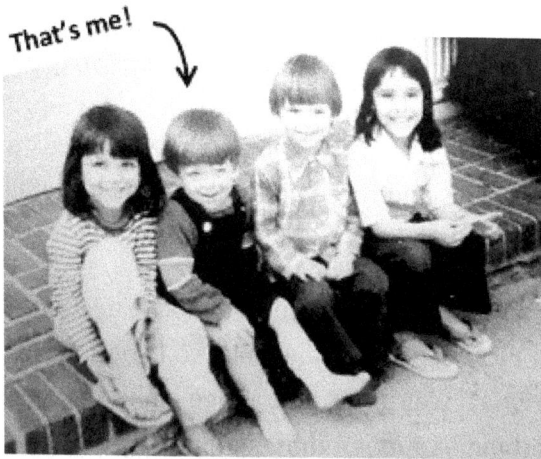

That's me!

CHAPTER 4

My Past Does NOT Define Me!

Most of the situations in my life have not gone the way I was hoping they would go. There are just too many factors for me control the outcomes.

I've realized looking back on my life, my whole journey ----- how many times God has been with me through it all. Because of that, I can no longer, in good conscious, ignore His Presence in my life.

There's no question about it, everything happens for a reason. I'm now convinced that there are NO accidents. I don't believe in accidents anymore.

*"Coincidence is merely God
choosing to remain anonymous."*

I grew up on Long Island, in a family with six kids ---
-- three boys and three girls. We were kind of like
The Brady Bunch.

I had a great childhood up until about age eight
and a half. I was a middle child, so I got a lot of
love, which was great. But at age eight and a half,
something happened that changed my entire
world.

My mother filed for a divorce.

She could no longer live in a negative environment
with my father. She had her reasons.

What I've learned today is that I cannot judge
either of my parents. They did the best they could
with what they had at that time. This has been a
very valuable lesson for me, in all areas of my life.

I don't have to judge others.

I don't have to condemn others. I don't have to feel
like the world is attacking me. I think the world is
merely just surviving. Everyone is just doing the
best they can to get through their own personal
messy worlds. Many are still living in their pasts.

There's no blame here but when my mom and dad went through their very chaotic divorce, it was a hostile environment for us kids.

It was angry. There was a lot of hatred. There was too much name-calling, cursing and just saying things to each other that no child should have to sit and hear.

Then it got even worse.

My parents started a battle against one another trying to win over each of us kids. Now, they were thinking about custody.

It was like a chess game and we were the pawns.

At the end of it all, we were marched into a busy courtroom and each child had to go up on the witness stand. The only recognizable faces in the room were mom and dad, but everyone else was strangers.

It was my turn to go up.

Dad was on the left. Mom was on the right.

Then the State Attorney asked me, *"Which parent do you want to spend the rest of your life with?"*

WTF!?!"

That is a very, very scarring question to ask an eight and a half year old boy, especially in that cold, unfriendly environment.

I remember looking out into the courtroom at my Dad, and seeing his sad puppy-dog-face. Then looking at my Mom and seeing her sad puppy-dog-face. Both their facial expressions were pleading, *"Pick me, pick me."*

Under the harsh white fluorescent lights, I felt sick to my stomach.

I felt like my world was crashing down around me. Everything I had ever known was disappearing before my eyes. I wanted it to stop. Someone make it go away. Why is this happening? Is this really happening? What the heck is happening?

I was so afraid and felt all alone up on the stand a million miles away from all the loving memories of my childhood.

[As I write these words, it has just been revealed to me that it was in that very moment ---- up on the stand at age eight and a half ---- when my fear of speaking in front of groups first cemented itself to me and its deep roots took hold of my life.]

I like to say my mom was the better marketer.

She marketed to my little boy *wants* rather than to my little boy *needs.*

Dad promised what every boy *needs*... rules, structure and discipline. But my mom promised what every boy *wants*... unlimited candy, TV and freedom.

I was a sharp kid, so I chose to live with my mom. Four of us chose my mom; two of us chose my dad.

Our lives would never be the same after that.

Somehow my brothers, sisters and I suppressed all our happy childhood memories deep in the back of our minds and in the deepest part of our hearts.

Still to this day, I do not remember all of our loving years of being a family before the messy divorce.

I now understand that young children don't have developed "filters "yet. Meaning, children don't know how to process big "adult" things like divorce.

Instead, what kids do is go into survival mode. In survival mode, children do whatever they think will help them to stay alive. They'll pretend it's not happening. They'll erase the past. They'll do whatever they need to just to survive the situation.

Period.

Many children survive by suppressing things into their subconscious. They act like it's not really happening and that's exactly what I did.

Unfortunately, along with all the BAD, I suppressed all the GOOD. My whole childhood, including my entire foundation of who I am and where I came from, was now gone forever. All of the love that was there before my parents divorced was locked deep down in some remote part of my mind and heart.

My early childhood felt like a lie.

It has taken many years to restore the relationships with my mom and dad, and to forgive them. Most importantly, I had to stop blaming them for my life not turning out the way I wanted.

I think many people reading this right now can relate to that. Maybe you grew up in a situation that was extremely painful. Maybe there was verbal abuse, like I had. Maybe there was physical abuse. Maybe there was sexual abuse.

Some of you reading this have suffered through horrible things, and with your permission, I'd like to say four things to you:

1) **IT SUCKS!** It sucks that it happened to you.
2) What happened to you was completely WRONG.
3) You're NOT to blame at all. Whoever did that to you, took your trust at a very early age. Like so many people, they were going through their own messed up things in their life and unfortunately took it out on you.
4) The most important thing to remember is this. The situations that happened to you, DO NOT define you. Situations do not define you. Your past does not define you. What defines you is how you use your past to better your future.

Again, what defines you is how you use your past to better your future.

We are all unique in so many things, but in our struggles, we are all the same.

Girls, you're all the same. You all fight with the same darn issues. I've seen it so many times, with so many of my female friends.

Men, we all battle with the exact same issues, too. What's amazing is that we think we are completely unique in our struggles, so we don't share what we are conflicted with because we think, "Someone may not like me, may not accept me or think I'm odd."

You're not odd or weird. The people around you are battling the same things you are. Most people don't share these things because they think they'll be judged, they won't be accepted or loved.

Everyone's living in fear and FEAR IS A LIAR.

However, the second you open up and share a struggle you're going through, something magical happens. Everyone starts to open up as well!

By being vulnerable enough to share your weaknesses, you give others permission to share theirs.

I've heard things like, "Oh my gosh, you went through that? I've gone through that. Or, I'm going through that now. How did you get through it? Or here's what I did and it worked!"

Look in the mirror.

You are now looking at the person responsible for your happiness.

PRINCIPLE #5:

*You are NOT defined by
what happened in your past.*

You choose your future. You can't change your
past, but you can choose your present, and it's
your present that defines your future.

So why did horrible things happen to you? I don't
know. But I do know that I've seen many people
take the very pain they went through as a child and
use it to serve others who are struggling with the
same pain. And that is a beautiful thing to watch.

*I believe that God turns our struggles into STORIES
that heal, our pain into POWER that conquers, and
our trials into TRIUMPHS that last.*

Once you realize that your past is just a story...it no
longer has any power over you. No matter what
happened to you, God still has a perfect plan for
your life.

Don't let your
history interfere
with your destiny.
– Dr. Steve Maraboli

Pain Can Be a Kick-Ass Motivator!

Growing up, we were the poorest family on the block, which unfortunately made me the poorest kid in the neighborhood. We had the worst looking home on the block and I was made fun of a lot because of it.

To this day I still remember my next-door neighbor. He was an African-American boy who was adopted by a white family. His family was fairly well to do and I remember his mom would always buy him the latest toys, gadgets, and technology. He always had the best of everything; clothing, brands, and styles.

I think it was his foster mother's way of loving him for what he had gone through before he was adopted. I can understand that now, but I didn't understand that back when I was a kid.

Back then all I knew was he was an annoying little punk who was constantly flashing his stuff in my face and making fun of me in front of all our friends.

He'd say things like, *"Poor Joseph, poor boy on the block. Why are you dressed like that? You're such a loser. How could you dress like that? Did you even take a shower today?"*

All my friends would laugh and it made me feel horrible. This happened almost every day.

Then I stopped being a victim.

Eventually, I began to build some muscle, and I would no longer take it. I stood up for myself.

For a while, it became a daily pattern where he would insult me (or my family, or my mom) and I would beat him up. I would physically beat him up and send him home crying every day.

I realize now that it was wrong to beat him up but, at the time, it sure felt good! I had finally stood my ground and wouldn't take his verbal abuse anymore.

Raised by a single mother on welfare, I dreaded our weekly trips to the supermarket and hung my head in shame as my Mom paid for the family's groceries with Food Stamps.

I secretly made a commitment to myself that when I became a man, my life would be different ----- I refused to ever be poor again.

I would be happy, healthy and wealthy.

That sparked a drive inside of me to start learning about business.

In my young mind, business was simply a "vehicle" to wealth; a way to change my life for the better so that it would never look the same again.

I started working every job I could. When I got bored, I move on to the next one. And I often got bored.

As it came time for college, my dad made us kids a pretty sweet deal ----- work one year (one summer) in the family business with him and he would pay for four years of college for each of us.

Sweet deal, right?!

My dad worked his tail off doing blue-collar, manual labor to provide for his six kids and had started a residential window cleaning business on the north shore of Long Island, NY.

My older siblings took advantage of my dad's generous offer and went off to colleges that cost tens of thousands of dollars a year. My father paid their tuitions and they earned their degrees.

I, on the other hand took a different route. I had an early entrepreneurial drive and didn't want to wait to graduate college in order to start making money.

It really didn't make sense to me.

It wasn't until years later when I was 25 years-old that I finally went to college but on my own terms.

I didn't want a degree, (a piece of paper), I wanted to take classes and educate myself in things that interested me. So, I signed up for <u>all</u> electives.

I took Latin dance class and acting. I took Aikido and martial arts. I attended business management and other classes about how to start and grow a business. That was it.

Still to this day, I don't have a full degree. I'm a few credits shy of an Associate's Degree. But that hasn't stopped me. Ironically, colleges hire me to come in and give lectures on entrepreneurship to their entrepreneurial students.

What's interesting about not having a degree is that it really hasn't held me back in life, especially in business.

I create businesses. That's what I do. I employ myself. But in between businesses or in the early stages of starting one, I'll often go out and get a nine-to-five-JOB just to pay the bills.

Surprisingly, I have been hired literally for every job I have ever applied for. More than 50% of the time, I didn't even bring a resume. Many times I didn't meet their requirements for the position, such as the wrong education, or no experience.

I just had me and that was enough.

In those earlier days, I was able to talk my way out of any situation, or into any situation.

I came into interviews with raw confidence and quickly learned to speak about what employers were looking for.

Want the secret to getting hired every time?

In an interview the #1 thing employers want to know is, "What's in it for them?" They can meet you. They can talk to you. They can listen to you. They can ask you questions about yourself. But all they are really hearing in the back of their head, all that's playing in their mind, is one simple question:

"What's in it for me? What's in it for me, talking with you right now? What's in it for me, taking your business card, right now? What's in it for me, hiring you right now? What's in it for me, paying for this product right now?"

Every human being in every situation is pre-wired to ask this same question. Heck you even asked it the first time you picked up this book.

"What's in it for me, to read this book?"

Everyone's asking the same question.

Remember the first time you asked out that pretty girl? Guess what she was asking herself? *"What's in it for me, going out with him?"*

You did it too.

Before you walked up to her, you asked yourself, *"What's in it for me, going out with her?"*

We are all narcissistic. Understanding that this question is on everyone's mind 24 hours a day, will give you an unfair advantage.

<u>PRINCIPLE #6</u>:

When you are looking to partner with someone, speak to their needs FIRST before your own.

Here's the #1 secret to
marketing ------>>>

*Always speak about,
"What's in it for them?"
BEFORE you speak about,
"What's in it for you?*

Adopting this simple principle
can EXPLODE your results!

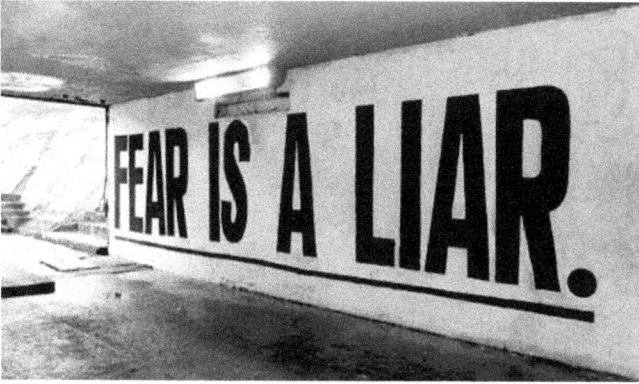

CHAPTER 5

How I Crushed the #1 Fear in The World – And You Can Too!

In high school I had to take a public speaking class. I was dreading the first day because speaking in front of a group scared me to death.

Of course, when I walked in, it was 90% girls.

The only thing worse than speaking in front of a group of people, is speaking in front of a group of attractive girls.

I remember our teacher. He was a tall, handsome, muscular guy that all the girls cooed over.

He loved being in the spotlight and exuded confidence. All the boys wanted to be like him.

Our first assignment was to write and recite a poem. My poem was about women. It started off something like, *"A woman is a masterpiece, a sculpture made of stone. No other creature can compare, in beauty she stands alone."*

I know corny, right? But it got a really great response from all the girls, applause and everything.

The sad part was that I was in a complete state of panic the entire time I was talking. My eyes were all stingy and watering and I was overly self-conscious; I was shaking the whole time I was speaking.

Then at the end, the teacher made a sarcastic comment. He said with a condescending stare, *"Oh look. We have another Walt Disney in the class. Joseph, one Disney is enough."*

It was an immature thing to say but because it came from someone I though highly of, it was very damaging and intensified my fear.

From then on, I tried to avoid every type of public speaking opportunity.

Years later in one of my businesses, I had a team of 50 people I had to get up in front of every morning and give a sales training/ motivational talk to "fire them up".

I fought through my public speaking fear every single time I went up. I've heard it said that we never conquer our fear; we just learn to manage it.

For many years that's what I did. I learned to live with *my fear*. But it was painful, and it wasn't until years later that I realized most people are deathly afraid public speaking. Like me, they just live with the fear. They keep it bottled up inside, hoping that no one will see it.

I soon realized fear was preventing me from my dreams and was holding me back in many areas of my life. I didn't want to get comfortable living with agonizing fear; I wanted to LOVE public speaking. I wanted to be excited to go up on stage.

But I didn't know how.

I started doing online research and Googled things like "how to get rid of public speaking fear." As I read through the abundance of articles and self-help advice, I found none that talked about how to remove the fear. They all taught how to manage it.

That really ticked me off.

Finally, I found one article that spoke about different limiting belief systems that are going on in the back of our heads. It said that fear is created deep in our subconscious mind.

I had never heard this before.

As I read through more articles, I began picking out the bits and pieces that I liked and started compiling them into a document that I named: "The 10 Commandments of Public Speaking."

*** You can find them here: ***
www.JosephWarren.net/products

When it was done, I read it aloud over and over and over for a few days. I felt like something small had changed in me.

By repeatedly reading through these new empowering belief systems, I was able to muster up enough courage to sign up for a Toastmasters group (an international organization that supports people's growth in public speaking skills).

That was my first step toward freedom.

For my first assignment I had to give a two minute "ice breaker" speech about myself.

As expected, I forced myself to push through the fear. But their encouragement was helpful. When I was done, I remember people complimenting me, and telling me I was a natural. I was dumbfounded and flattered, but I was still scared.

NOTE: I think Toastmaster groups serve a great purpose because it helps you get through the *initial* steps of becoming a better speaker.

I remember speaking with the top speaker in our group (she was a super engaging and confident speaker). I asked her how she did it. She replied, *"You want to know my secret?"*

Of course I did!

"Well, if I'm speaking to an audience of total strangers…. then I'll have one drink."

Huh?

She continued, *"If it's an audience of my colleagues who know me, then I'll have two drinks."*

I thought she was kidding, until she held up a metal flask full of alcohol! WTF!?

The top speaker in the group and she drank alcohol to cope with and manage her fear. Ugh!

She insisted, *"Listen, everyone has public speaking fear. No one ever conquers it. It's just part of life. All you can do learn to manage it."*

But that wasn't good enough for me. That was her limiting belief system, not mine.

I wanted to conquer my speaking fear ----- crush it ----- so I could be excited and passionate when speaking in front of large audiences like one of my all-time heroes did.

For many years, Tony Robbins was a role model of mine. He was charismatic, passionate and full of energy. That's what I wanted and darn it, that's what I would get!

Did you know that before every talk Tony has given for the last 20 years he chants the same mantra to get himself psyched up?

It starts like this, *"I now command my subconscious mind to direct me in helping as many people as possible to better their lives by given me..."*

*** You can read the rest here: ***
www.JosephWarren.net/products

Although I still had debilitating fear, it wasn't until a few years later that I was able to find a real solution. It was a five hour DVD program that cost me $200. That was the best $200 I ever spent!

The program walked me through dealing with the 16 most common childhood belief systems in all of humanity.

It taught that before age seven, our belief systems are shaped by those closest to us: parents, family, friends, school environments, etc. We form belief systems about the world and reality around us.

Here's where it gets scary.

The same belief systems that we had as children, we carry into our adult lives. Good and bad. What once helped us as children may now limit us as adults.

Limiting belief systems negatively affect many areas of our adult lives. For example, why are we afraid to speak in front of two or more people, when we are totally confident speaking in front of one? Why is that? It's not logical at all.

Why do we get nervous and change our behavior when a video camera goes on and we see a little flashing red light?

Why do we forget who we are and what we already know? Why do we freeze up?

This program walked me through those kinds of questions and gave me new empowering belief systems. It permanently scratched the "record' of limited beliefs that had been playing in my subconscious mind for nearly my whole life.

I think the one thing we need to do as human beings before we die is to remove all of our limiting beliefs and character defects. We all have them; they match the environments we grew up in. I think the more of them we can remove by the time we die, the more value we add to the world. It's that simple.

Although the DVD program had a hefty price, I decided that continuing to live with this fear would be a greater price to pay.

As I sat in front of my computer, I asked myself if it was worth it. Were my dreams worth $200?

Are yours?

*** You can find the DVD here: ***
www.JosephWarren.net/products

I bought it and watched it. Two weeks later I had a talk. When I was finished presenting, someone came up and asked me how I learned to speak so confidently and effortlessly.

"He's asking me?" I thought. He sounded just like me when I would ask other people! I thought about how to respond for a second. Then I said, *"Thanks, but I'm not really sure."*

It was in that moment that I realized that I hadn't even thought once about being scared. Something had changed in me on a subconscious level.

For the first time in my life, I didn't dread the upcoming talk. I didn't give myself pep talks to get through it, like I had done so many times before. Honestly, I forgot about the talk until the day before. From that day forward, I was free from public speaking fear!

Now I absolutely LOVE speaking in front of groups. Just like Tony Robbins, I now get excited about it. I'm passionate about it. I crushed the #1 fear in the world and it feels great!

You can too. When you remove fear from your life, you are free to do what you are meant to do in the world.

Imagine walking around with heavy chains, trying to succeed. Try running a 10K marathon with a 100 pound dumbbell attached to your ankle. Let me know how successful you're going to be. What if you could find a hot torch gun and burn right through that metal chain and free yourself, how well are you going to do now?

The results are "night and day". Now apply that same metaphor to any area of your life that you have fear.

<u>FACT</u>: You must break free from fear.

I believe that behind your greatest fear, lies your greatest passion—that which is going to bring you ultimate happiness and inner joy. Until you face your fear head on and walk through its door, you will never experience your full potential in life.

Nowadays, when something scares me (and simultaneously excites me), I know I need to do it —even if I don't know how to yet. I need to take the next step. I just do the next right thing.

Most people are walking around functioning at only 10% of their full potential, because the other 90% of their potential is sleeping with fear.

When you remove all the "skadooze" (my word for anything nasty, yucky, evil, garbage, crap, etc.), you become open to the right mindset and soon attract the right skill sets.

Sometimes in life you have those rare opportunities where there are outside forces (friends, family, etc.) pushing you to do what you know you need to do, but you don't have the strength or the courage to do it on your own because the fear is just so overwhelming.

I've seen people temporarily succeed because they had a great team of supporters who helped push them over the first hurdle, and sometimes the second and third. The first victory gave them a little confidence, on the second it started to build, and by the third, they were running on momentum.

Soon they started doing really cool things.

But what happened when they lost their great supporters? They plateaued and now could see areas of their life where they were no longer getting great results.

This is common with top celebrities who made it all the way up on talent and momentum, and then all of a sudden they start "sucking wind."

Why? Is it because one day they woke up and lost their talent or their skillset? That's absurd, right?

It's because their core, limiting belief systems from childhood had never been fully removed. They may look fearless, but it was actually outside forces that were pulling them out of their darkness. But the darkness still existed within.

TRUTH: Until you target your inner darkness and face it head on, where it's no longer there because you shined so much light onto it, your permanent transformation won't happen.

I can honestly say that I have been permanently transformed. How do I know? Because it doesn't matter how long I go without giving a talk ----- the second I hit the stage ----- I have zero fear and nail it every time.

I recently was sharing a story with a friend of mine about being on stage, when she stopped me and said that she noticed my body language (physiology) had instantly changed; my shoulders pulled back and I was "locked in."

"You owned it." she said. *"It was like you were still on stage. It became part of you. And you're fired-up and passionate as if you're re-living it."*

I wasn't even aware that I was doing that. But she was right because when I'm up on stage, I feel unstoppable! I'm 100% percent in my "flow" when I'm up there speaking—more than any other time in my life, throughout my day, or whatever. Sitting here writing this book is cool. It's great. But when I'm writing, I'm not really in my flow. Speaking is my flow. It's what I do and I do it well.

Helping people conquer their fear and unlock their full potential, that's something I'm passionate about. When I look into someone's eyes, into their soul, and help them to see who they really are—it's phenomenal. Nothing can touch that feeling for me.

As we remove fear from our lives, we are now free to do what we are meant to do in the world -----
and that changes everything.

PRINCIPLE #7:

Behind your greatest fear, lies your greatest passion and until you face it head on and walk through its door, you will never unleash the greatness that lies within you.

"God uses the good, the
bad, the ugly, and the
beautiful from
our past to paint the
dreams of our future."

Joseph Warren

"I'M OM A MISSION TO HELP AS MANY PEOPLE AS POSSIBLE TO BETTER THEIR LIVES AND POSITIVELY IMPACT THE WORLD."

Joseph Warren

CHAPTER 6

Hard-Wired For Success!

As CEO of CoCreativ I have two co-founders, Heather and Jason. Both joined me in a previous consulting company I started.

When we first met we had three different stories, three different perspectives: three different personalities, three different childhoods, three different belief systems, three sets of eyes looking out at the world around us.

This can cause serious conflicts, which is why team dynamics and relationships are so difficult.

Relationships require work because what you see and what I see are two different things based on how our lives have gone so far.

So there we were (the three of us) trying to build a business together and I knew immediately we had to learn to communicate better.

So I did what I do with all new problems I encounter. I did some research to find successful solutions that someone else has already proven.

I don't model mediocrity. I model peak performance. I want to know who is already crushing it and getting the results I want.

In my search, I came across a phenomenal online assessment test. It is a profiling system, but very unique in that it identifies eight entrepreneurial skill sets and strengths.

The deeper I dug, the more depth I found. It was like a rabbit hole and I had just swallowed the "red pill". It was based on 400 years of studying different cultures.

When it came to working with Heather and Jason, rather than being defensive and resistant toward their perspectives, wouldn't it be better if I could understand how they are "naturally wired"?

What were their dominant strengths that were essential to my team?

$100.00 seemed a little expensive for a 20 minute online test, so again I found myself questioning if it would be worth it.

Let's do it. I decided to test it on myself first.

*** You can find it here: ***
www.JosephWarren.net/products

As I read through the material, I resonated with the CREATOR profile because according to the test, CREATORS love to innovate and make things better.

I often seen flaws in the way things are currently being done and come up with better ways to do them. Clearly, I was a CREATOR.

But upon completion, the test results said that my dominant entrepreneurial profile was STAR and CREATOR was my secondary profile.

I remember saying to myself, *"I just spent $100 and they gave me the wrong profile. I want a refund"*.

So that's what I did. I sent them an email saying my test results were wrong and I wanted a refund.

They responded with, *"Joseph, we hear this all the time. What we find is 50% of the people that take our test think the results are correct. The other 50% think they're really a different profile and want a refund because they don't agree with the test results. The truth is you aren't getting the optimal results you want in life because you've been practicing your secondary strength instead of your DOMINANT strength. We will gladly refund your money, that's not even a question. However, can we ask you to do one thing? Try on your STAR profile. Practice some of the strategies we recommend and if it still doesn't resonate with you, we'll gladly give you your money back."*

Challenge accepted.

As I took a closer look at the STAR profile, I started to see the truth: while I'm good at creating "better mousetraps", I'm actually better at selling them. STARS tend to be great sales people.

Because I had practiced my secondary strength of creating solutions, businesses, and ideas for so long, I mistakenly thought I was <u>great</u> at it.

I wasn't.

When STARS shine, people follow.

A good example would be Oprah Winfrey. She doesn't sell her own products, instead she shines her light (her personality), her STAR power on other people's products. Wherever she shines her light, people flock. That's why when Oprah would recommend a book on her show, a million people would run out and buy it.

Could it be true that I was a STAR???

I read that for STARS to be effective, they have to become great at public speaking.

Are you kidding me?!

What I had been avoiding my entire life (and had just conquered), was the very skillset that I needed in order to shine and become one of the best in the world at what I was naturally wired to do.

I started to see how God was leading me towards His purpose for my life. When I got out of the way and just accepted that I could be wrong and did the next right thing, doors started to open.

Once I owned my STAR profile, I looked back on my life and I thought, "Okay, all the books I've ever read, all the people I've really resonated with... which profile were they?"

Tony Robbins...Oprah Winfrey...top speakers and performers? They were all STAR profiles. The more I tried it on, the more it started to fit.

Long story short, I let them keep the money. It was probably the second best $100 I've ever spent.

I now believe that one of the most important things a business person should do is to identify their DOMINANT entrepreneurial profile.

When you practice within your dominant strengths, you get peak performance results, as opposed to just mediocre results.

You know that feeling when you're doing something and you just know your nailing it? You get the tingles and you just know you were meant to do this? You're excited and scared at the same time because what you're doing is bigger than you are?

It's called working in your flow.

After you face your greatest fear, BOOM, you find your greatest passion. You walk through that door, you take it on and that's the first step. Then you must practice, practice, and practice some more.

When you practice what you were created to do, you're going to outshine all the other people who don't have your same dominant strength. You're going to have an unfair advantage over all your peers and colleagues.

Why?

Not because you're any better than them, it's because you're naturally wired in an area that they are not.

They may be good at what you do but they will never be as good as you.

They can become great at what they were meant to do but first they must conquer their fear. And how many people do you think will actually do what it takes to reach their full potential?

Only a few, it's sad but true.

But YOU, my friend, you will become the best in the world at what you were predestined to do. Only YOU can do it.

Now I had to know what Jason and Heather's profiles were so I could better communicate with them and know what to expect from them.

Jason was a MECHANIC profile. MECHANICS don't build the widget and they don't sell it either. They build the systems and processes around the widget that make it duplicable and scalable. Interesting.

McDonald's Ray Crock was a MECHANIC profile. He discovered a little restaurant in the middle of California that had a great concept. He knew it needed to be everywhere across the U.S. and he knew he could take it there. He bought the franchise rights and that's what he did. He came in as a MECHANIC and started duplicating every tiny process by creating little systems around everything, all the way down to how long it took to cook perfect French Fries.

That's what Jason is gifted to do. He does all the tedious stuff I hate, and sometimes, he'd complain about it because it was new to him or he felt like I was trying to get out doing stuff. He was right, I was.

I was trying to get out of doing stuff that I'm not suited for.

My time is reserved for my skill set alone, so I can keep getting better and better and sharper and sharper at what I was meant to do.

The world sells us this ideology in school and business, that if you're bad at something (your weakness), you need to practice it until you get better.

That's actually 100% backwards.

You're never going to be the best in the world at your weaknesses. However, what's that one thing that you're naturally already good at?

Spend all your time and energy on that—and you'll become the best in the world at it. That's the key.

Even though Jason resisted many times, I kept pushing MECHANIC on him. I want him to become one of the best in the world at it.

"Keep practicing. Keep swinging the bat. You don't feel it yet? That's okay. It's coming."

Heather is a SUPPORTER profile. SUPPORTERS are naturally gifted at serving others. They are phenomenal in a team environment. They support everyone and make sure all team members have what they need in order to be successful.

Ironically enough, STARS (like me) require strong SUPPORTERS beside them. Why? Because STARS tend to be selfish and somewhat full of themselves.

When they're lit up, people are naturally drawn to them. This makes them feel important and inflates their ego.

I've had to learn a lot of humility in that area.

SUPPORTERS are great at lining up with STARS and helping them to shine and be their best. In doing so, the SUPPORTER is doing what they absolutely love to do—serving and helping others.

If that sounds like a self-less role to you that's because it is. But that's exactly what gets SUPPORTERS all tingly inside.

The bottom line is this. When you practice your core strengths and surround yourself with others who are practicing theirs, your team can operate at peak performance.

Plus you stop stepping on each other's toes.

One of the greatest benefits of taking the profile test is that it doesn't just make you realize what your strengths are, but also what your weaknesses are.

When you know what your weaknesses are, you know when to say "NO".

Say "NO" to all the shiny opportunities and "YES" to only the things that complement your natural wiring, because those will lead you to peak performance.

Everything else is a waste of your time, energy and resources.

PRINCIPLE #8:

You're never going to be the best in the world at your weaknesses. Focus all of your time, energy, and resources on practicing your natural strengths.

*** You can find the test here: ***
www.JosephWarren.net/products

JOSEPH M. WARREN

> HARDSHIPS OFTEN
> PREPARE ORDINARY
> PEOPLE FOR AN
> EXTRAORDINARY
> DESTINY...
>
> —C.S. LEWIS

CHAPTER 7

How Forgiveness Set Me Free!

It's not enough to identify your childhood limiting beliefs, you must REMOVE them. This means that you'll have to make amends with family members.

WARNING: This chapter is not for wimps.

I used to think I was unique in that I was the only child who suffered through a terrible divorce. I was wrong.

ALL families are broken in some way.

If you're jacked up in the head and the heart from childhood, guess what? You're not alone.

More than HALF the world is full of broken kids who grew up to be broken adults.

But don't you want to free yourself from your childhood baggage?

You'll have to man up, own it, and work through it. If you leave it stuck inside, it will eat you from within.

Let's get started.

Can you acknowledge that your parents did the best they could with what they had at the time?

They didn't know any better. They were raised by parents who also were jacked up, and their parents' parents were jacked up. Limiting beliefs are passed down from one generation to another.

The question is....will you be that one person in your family who breaks the cycle? Will you put an end to it in your generation, so that you're not passing on these limiting belief systems to your children? Seriously, will you?

Have you ever wondered why the world is so jacked up? This is why. It's filled with jacked up kids who became adults who are now raising their own jacked up kids and passing on these belief systems. That's the core problem with society. Broken families mean broken society. However, we don't all have to remain broken like this. It's a decision.

Once you learn, identify and accept that you're not alone and your parents did they best they could with what they had, you can let go and release it.

You can forgive.

Forgiveness is a very dangerous word to some people. Forgive. "What do you mean forgive? I don't want to forgive! They are wrong. They messed up my life. I'm screwed up because of my parents."

Do you want the truth? You're not a screwed up adult because of your parents. You have a stronger character because of the struggles that you had to go through because of your parents own selfish decisions.

However, if you're a screwed up adult, it's only because of one person—and that's you.

Are you a person who's refusing to forgive and take full, complete, 100% responsibility for your life and your actions going forward?

Let go of it.

Let go of blaming others. It's only holding YOU back. The first step to breaking the cycle is admitting your brokenness and forgiving yourself. First you forgive yourself for how you turned out, and then you take full responsibility for your life starting tomorrow.

For example, I went to my mom and dad and asked them to make amends to us kids for what we went through during the divorce. Was it right for me to ask them to make amends for their wrongdoing?

I believe it was so I did. It was the right thing to do for my siblings. We needed healing and my parents held the key that could set us free.

However, there's a very fine line. I had to do it from a loving, not condemning, place. Again, mom and dad did the best they could with what they had. Nobody taught them how to parent. So could they have known what damage a divorce would cause in their children.

I spoke with my dad first because my mom was a little more emotionally fragile. My dad was a Marine who survived Vietnam so I knew he could take what I had to say.

I spoke to him as gently as I could and said, *"Dad, I've got to say this...and I'm not condemning you in any way, I understand that you did the best you could at the time and with what you knew. However, I got hurt and scarred because of the divorce and so did my brothers and sisters... your children. Again, I'm not condemning, but I need you to own that. I need you to take responsibility for that. I need you to release all of us from that. And the way to release all of us is to: One, acknowledge it happened. Two, ask us for forgiveness. It's not about you. It's about the kids that you love. It's about setting them free so we can heal. If you could do that, Dad, this family, your family, is going to change forever."*

This caught him off guard and, as you can imagine, he didn't take it too well at first. I remember seeing his physiology and body language change abruptly. His right hand clenched up into a fist.

He got red in the face and said, *"Son! What do you want me to do? Admit I was a bad father? Is that what you want?!?!"*

I said, *"No, Dad. That's not what I want. However, if you don't man up and do this right now, and I mean this with all respect, if you don't acknowledge what your children went through...*

the pain that was caused to us through your
actions and mom's actions at the time, and you
don't ask for forgiveness and set us free? Then yes,
Dad, you're not a good father."

He did everything he could to not swing at me.

I said, "Dad, you do whatever you feel is the right
thing to do and I'm not going to say another word.
It's up to you. But you needed to know what's
going on in your children. Because I don't think
you've really seen the residue of the divorce.
Maybe you thought everyone is okay. We're not.
Dad, we're all broken. You can set us free and help
us to heal."

He just walked away.

My sister heard that I upset my Dad. She got
agitated with me because she thought I created
unnecessary tension and conflict. She was upset I
ruined the family picnic.

Sometimes in life, especially in our families, we
need to "man up" regardless of where or when.
And if you're a woman, you need to "woman up".
Go face the giant "elephant" in the room and stop
hiding behind its shadow, acting like everything's
alright. It's not. Call it out.

Yes, you may be ostracized. You may be disliked in the moment. And I was. I quickly became very unpopular in my family for the next month or so.

However, it was a month later that I received a letter in the mail from my father. He had photocopied it and sent it to each of his children. The letter was him acknowledging his part in our childhood, apologizing and asking for forgiveness so that we could heal.

My Dad set us free.

This gave me an amazing respect, compassion and love for my father because I knew how difficult it was for him to do. What he did is something very few fathers will do... he put himself in a weaker position than his children. He became subject to his kids and he empowered them.

As Mohammed Ghandi says, "Be the change you want to see in the world." As I say, be the change you want to see in your family. Stand up.

Until you free yourself and have peace in who you are and where you come from, you cannot fully shine. You cannot fully live out your full potential. You cannot fully be you. So you must have healing within the family.

Be firm, but loving and humble. It will be difficult and it will scare you, but remember that behind your greatest fear lies your greatest passion and your greatest joy...that very thing that's going to make you the most happy.

Behind that big ass elephant in the room that's keeping your family divided, broken, unforgiving, and non-compassionate to each other is the love, joy, and family life you've always wanted.

Man up.

There are some situations out there where one or both parents may be absent, for whatever reason. What I recommend in these situations is to, first, set yourself free. But then you still have to set others free.

I've seen different exercises where people in counseling sessions let go and get the healing they need from an absent parent figure by putting an empty chair in front of them, closing their eyes and visualizing their parent, or whomever it is they needed healing with.

When they open their eyes they are literally picturing them, believing that they're in that chair in front of them and then saying what they've always wanted to say. Sometimes it starts out very angry and hostile. If that's what is needed, well, it's actually a perfect situation because you're not going to offend anyone.

Get it out. Project it on mom or dad who's fictitiously sitting in that chair. Say everything. Say whatever. It may be too late for mom or dad to come back into your life, but that's okay. You must still express it. You need to get it out for you. You need healing first.

After you forgive yourself, you may need to go to someone and ask them for forgiveness for your wrongdoing. And that's never easy. But if you say you love them, then you will.

You may be a parent now who needs to go to their eight year old boy or girl and ask for forgiveness because you have passed on to them some serious childhood belief systems that are very limiting to their future. And then, from this day forward, you need to own up and change that by instilling new uplifting ones in them.

Or maybe there's someone else in your family you've wronged and haven't spoken to in 10 years, 20 years, or 40 years. It's never too late.

Forgiveness is the key that will set you free.

Whether it's others who need to forgive you, or people you need forgiveness from. In both situations, you must forgive yourself first. Then ask them for forgiveness. Then forgive them.

Accept that you're not alone in your brokenness (EVERY PERSON ON THE PLANET IS BROKEN) Just let go and release the anger and blame like I did.

When the blaming stops, the healing begins.

You can forgive.

"Whenever you stand praying, FORGIVE, if you have <u>anything</u> against <u>anyone</u>, so that your Father who is in Heaven will also forgive you YOUR transgressions. But if you <u>do not forgive</u>, neither will your FATHER who is in Heaven forgive your transgressions." ~ Mark 12:25

PRINCIPLE #9:

Until you free yourself and have peace about who you are and where you come from, you cannot fully shine.

PASSION # 3

Faith

"FAITH IS JUMPING WITHOUT KNOWING WHERE YOUR FEET WILL LAND... HOPE IS BELIEVING THAT NO MATTER HOW FAR YOU JUMP, YOU'LL ALWAYS LAND ON YOUR FEET."

#NoRegrets

© 2014 Joseph Warren

Co™

JOSEPH M. WARREN

CHAPTER 8

The Billionaire
Who Changed My Life!

About 12 months ago, I was working hard on improving our business model for CoCreativ because we weren't getting much traction.

I remember spending a lot of time working on side projects just to pay the bills. Money was insanely tight, and when it came to my faith (something I hold very dear), I was slacking miserably.

JOSEPH M. WARREN

Then something happened.

I felt a gentle prompting within me to draw closer to God. But I had so much stuff to do and I just kept thinking, "I don't have the time". But the prompting continued day-after-day.

I remember sending up a prayer, *"Lord, what is it?! What do You want from me? You know my busy schedule. You know I have bills to pay. Who's going to pay them? If You want me to get closer to You, then provide me with enough income to pay my bills and I will come spend time with You."*

That prayer was my FIRST step back to God.

It was about two weeks later when a buddy of mine pulled me aside and asked me to coach him on an area of his life where he was getting poor results. He offered to pay me.

I needed to make more money and he needed certain results over the next 30 days that I knew I could provide. It was a good deal for both of us.

I said, *"Sure I can help you but it has to be worth my time."* Then I dropped my large fee on him.

He gasped. *"Whoa! That's a lot of money!"*

I confidently replied, *"Yes and those are big goals*

you have! Do you really want these goals? How will your life change? What will your life look like 30 days from now, when you have what you want?"

He thought about for a minute and said, *"My life would be awesome! It would be amazing!"*

We both knew how much he wanted to hit these goals. He was happy with the other areas of his life but not this one. He had pain and could help him. After that realization, I said to him, *"Great, so your life is going to change 30 days from now, and it will never be the same...isn't that worth XXXXXXXXXX dollars to you?"*

Needless to say, he wrote me a check and I started coaching him. Two weeks in, he referred me to his friend who hired me to help him reach similar goals. After giving him the exact same pitch, he also wrote me a large check the next day.

(With 30 days, both gentlemen hit their goals.)

I now had enough money to take off work for the next eight months --- and that's exactly what I did!

I started spending money like it was going out of style. I flew to the Hamptons with some buddies who rented a huge eleven-bedroom home. Pool, tennis courts, the works. We partied for five days.

A week later, I partied some more at another rented house down in South Florida, right smack on the beach!

I was having so much fun partying that I completely forgot about God. Can you believe I totally ignored the fact that God had answered my prayer?!

He gave me the money and the extra time that I prayed for and here I was out spending it all over the place like a selfish little boy!

Finally I thought to myself, *"God did His end of the deal, now I need to man up and do mine."*

I went down to my local church and sat in the chapel with Him. My intentions were good but it was agonizing trying to sit there quietly and try to connect with the Creator of the universe!

Honestly, prayer was something I'd never been successful at doing. I've always been easily distracted. My mind just races all over the place and it's extremely difficult to quiet down the "noise" of the world.

For many people, the most difficult thing for them to do is to just shut down everything outside of them and center themselves. That's me.

My first attempt was terrible. It didn't last very long, maybe a few minutes here and there. I came back the next day and the same thing happened.

But I was resolved to try my best.

The third day, still the same thing. It took about a week of me painfully trying to quiet the noise and distractions and sit there quietly before I finally started discipline my mind.

Then God did something I wasn't expecting. He brought Godly role models into my life.

It started with my friend inviting me to some Christian worship service on a Tuesday night.

We walked into a large room with about 200 young people worshiping God through music.

It looked like some youth rally. It was totally different than what I was used to but I was open to it because there were at least a hundred pretty girls (that definitely kept me curious).

The best part was when the pastor invited some businessman up on stage to share his story.

This man shared how God turned his world upside down. He went from living a selfish life in pursuit of wealth to living a God-centered life in pursuit of

Heaven. What really struck me was when he started talking about how he now ran his business.

He owns a billion dollar company, and yes, that's billion with a "B". This guy is crushing it! His family owned a NFL football team at one time, and guess what?

Now he prays before every board meeting. He prays in the board meeting. He doesn't make a major decision for the company without first consulting God in his own quiet conversations.

Some of his employees think he's insane. He said some are atheists. Even though they're not all Christians, he holds no prejudice. It takes all types. Nevertheless, he's there to set an example. Not for show, but because that's who he is.

When a decision needs to be made, he talks with God, and then waits until he gets an answer. Then he knows exactly which way to move. With total confidence, he makes decisions.

Every single time he does this, they have record-breaking revenue come in. His company just keeps getting bigger and bigger because He completely puts his trust in the hands of God. He may be the boss to his employees, <u>but God is his boss</u>.

I had never heard of anyone doing this. I was fascinated. I was hooked.

He was speaking about combining his business with his faith. He called it *Marketplace Ministry*. That intrigued me.

Even more was that God was financially blessing him for doing so. You can't argue with success. He was a billionaire living out his Christian faith. I wanted to know more, I needed to know more.

I had to speak with him.

I walked over an introduced myself and told him I was interested in learning more about *Marketplace Ministry*. He replied by inviting me to join a men's leadership group he was starting, called *Experiencing God™*. How could I not?

That group was my SECOND step back to God.

This men's group opened the door for me to a more advance group for business leaders called *Lifework Leadership™*.

There I met a man whose program would change my life forever!

He was a guest speaker and he spoke about a program he had developed that promised to teach a person how to hear "the quiet whisper of God" in prayer. He said God wants to reveal Himself to each of us and show us His plan for our lives.

But more than that, God wants to reveal three things about us: our _Identity_ (not how we see ourselves, not how others see us, but how God sees us), our _Destiny_ (the amazing thing that God created us to do that no one else can do) and our _Assignment_ (the specific work that God wants us to do in the world).

Again, I was fascinated and knew I had to talk with him. As we chatted afterwards, he invited me to purchase his program but I told him that I didn't want to do it alone. This was too important to me. I wanted guaranteed results and asked if I could hire him to personally coach me through his 10-week program.

He agreed.

This program was my THIRD step back to God.

The program unpeeled more layers of how God wired me, such as my character strengths (and weaknesses) and my spiritual gifts.

Then at Week 8, something remarkable happened.

I was sitting in the chapel reading through the program and quietly waiting to hear from God. And that's when it happened.

God spoke to me.

The first time it happened, I didn't get much. I didn't hear much. I just heard a few words and broken phrases, but I wrote them down anyway. I read back over them, and while it made a little sense, really it didn't. But it was a start.

Was it just my imagination? I had to know.

I went back the next day with a little hope that maybe there was something there. Maybe I could learn what these guys had learned and mastered.

I got a few more phrases.

And then the next day, I think, a sentence; a full sentence. I came back day-after-day and the same thing...a little more, a little more...

I started to realize that my "spiritual hearing" was slowly improving because I was taking time out of my busy life to put God first, just like you would with a friend who you care about.

Every day I would return to the chapel and sit for one hour and every day I would hear just a little more than the day before. This was absolutely fascinating to me. It was surreal.

I was stoked because the Creator of the Universe was speaking with me?!

Was this really happening? It was crazy-exciting!

But was it really Him or just my mind playing some very sadistic trick on me?

The program taught me how to start writing and journaling what I'm hearing; word for word, to always record the conversations.

So I did. I wrote down in my journal every word God said and every word I said.

Every day I was given a little more. It was as though God was feeding me small digestible bites, as much as He knew I was ready for.

Spiritually, I was like a baby bird learning to eat.

As I read back over each conversation from the day before, I was convinced that this wasn't something my mind was making up. The conversations were real. They were intimate. And His answers had so much depth, far more than I did.

He told me things about myself that I never knew.

Each day He would reveal a little more about my Identity, a little more about my Destiny and a little more about my Assignment. He spoke about His perfect plan for my life.

But I still had doubts because God doesn't speak to His People anymore, right?

Maybe in the Bible but that was 2,000 years ago and even back then, God only spoke to a few chosen people like Moses, Abraham, and the Prophets.

Why would He be speaking to me, a selfish bad boy from Long Island? It just didn't make sense to me.

My whole life I never even had one single conversation with Him and now all of a sudden, I was speaking with Him almost every day (sometimes for a several hours)?!

But no matter how many doubts I had, <u>I knew it was God</u>. I felt His Presence all around me in that quiet chapel. I felt His love, the love of the Father.

Each conversation healed some part of my broken past. God was "loving on me" like a father does. He was comforting me. Why? Because He loves me. So why didn't He speak to me before? Then it hit me, I never pursued Him like this before. Earnestly.

"Pursue Me earnestly,
and I will reveal My Face to you."

<u>That was the answer</u>. For the first time in my life, I was determined to hear from Him, no matter how long it took, no matter how long I had to sit there. I had made a firm decision not to quit.

> *"Have faith in God. Truly I say to you, whoever says to this mountain, 'Be taken up and cast into the sea,' and <u>does not doubt in his heart</u>, but believes that what he says <u>is going to happen</u>, it will be granted him. Therefore I say to you, all things for which you pray and ask, <u>believe that you have received them</u>, and they will be granted you."*
> ~ Mark 12:22

God removed the mountain of doubt in my heart by bringing to me other men who could hear Him. They taught me how.

I put in the time, I put in the effort, and God did the rest. That's the secret.

Listen. You can't grow your relationship with your friend if you don't spend time together. It's the same thing with your Creator. You must spend time with Him, shutting down the world and the noise around you, and just sit quietly, and listen.

It's not about talking, that's the thing.

The way I used to always pray was, *"Lord, can you give me this? Can you fix this? Here's what's going on in my life. I've screwed up everything, can you come fix it?"*

I was always asking for stuff. My prayers were very self-centered. These gentlemen taught me how to pray more God-centered.

It's all about Him. It has nothing to do with us. Remove yourself from the picture, and sit with Him in silence. Find out <u>what He wants</u>:

1) Who does He say you are?
2) What purpose did He create you for?
3) What does He want you to do for Him?

The One who created you is the One who knows your future and has all the answers, so doesn't it make sense to go spend time with Him?

Sure you can continue chasing after happiness and trying to feel fulfilled from the temptations of the world like I did...whether that be through alcohol, drugs, addictions, sex, or some other sensual pleasure. But all these things leave you feeling empty and alone. Really you're just putting "Band-Aids" on a deeper problem.

If you are not connected with your Creator, you are chasing the wind.

All of a sudden my faith (religion) was more than just something I knew in my head. For the first time in my life, it was something I truly felt and believed in my heart.

Before then, I didn't even know I was missing that. It wasn't until these intimate conversations with God that I started to "experience" Him in my life.

Remember, before Moses led Israel out of Egypt, he was alone with God in the desert. Abraham was also with God in the desert. Even Jesus Himself, spent 40 days alone with God in the desert before starting His ministry.

There's something to that.

If you want God to show His Face to you and reveal His purpose for your life, you first must seek Him earnestly in the desert. The desert is anywhere away from the distractions of the world.

For me, the chapel was the desert where I found God. He and I alone ----- no distractions, no talking or asking for things, just me listening and waiting for Him to speak with me.

God requires your undivided attention.

So if you're sitting there like I used to be wondering why God doesn't speak to you, then ask yourself this, *"How much time do you spend with God in total quiet each day... 30 minutes... 20 minutes... 10 minutes... 5 minutes... 2 minutes?"*

That's your answer. You haven't put in the time.

Anyone who plays sports knows they have to put in the time, the effort, and the discomfort if they want to get better. They have to get comfortable with being uncomfortable.

Why do you think it's any different with God?

Listen. I get it. I used to be where you are, coming up with the same reasons why I didn't have the time.

Sundays I would go to church, and do the church thing and the God thing. Then in business, it was time to crush it! Get to the top, be successful, and climb the business ladder, whatever it takes.

Yet these gentlemen, whom God brought into my life, had somehow figured out a better way. They were able to bridge that disconnect between business and Faith. I wanted that.

I didn't want to live a double-life anymore. I was tired of being a *Bi-Polar Christian™.* The world is full of *Bi-Polar Christians™.* Are you one?

I wanted to be whole, complete and God-centered; the type of man that I saw in these guys.

So, I started spending time with them, and they started to teach me how to pray correctly; how to quiet my mind and hear the quiet whisper of God.

They helped me understand that God doesn't speak to us in an "audible voice". He speaks gently to His children in a quiet whisper.

If God spoke to us in some booming, God-sized audible voice...we wouldn't require any faith. Heck, then even atheists would believe in His existence.

I know it sounds crazy to anyone reading this, but hearing God's voice is totally possible. It sounded crazy to me too when I heard it the first time from these successful businessmen. But it's so true.

WARNING: The road back to God is simple but it's never easy. You'll have to shed your old habits and replace them with new ones. This takes work.

You'll have to surrender everything to God; your past, your present, and your future. No exceptions.

Remember, for me it all started because I prayed a very specific prayer back then and the Lord heard my heart and removed my excuses. My prayer was raw but sincere and God loves that.

He slowly built up my character and one-by-one, He removed my character flaws (I still have many but there's less than before).

He wants to do the same for you, but you must ask Him for it. God never interferes with your free will. That's His gift to you.

He wants you to come back to Him freely.

One hour per day with God, that's the secret.

If I paid you $1,000,000 dollars in cash, you would find the time to make it happen, true or false?

PRINCIPLE #10:

If you are not connected with your Creator, you are chasing the wind. Most situations are bigger than you, that's why you can't control them.

*** You can find his Program here: ***
www.JosephWarren.net/products

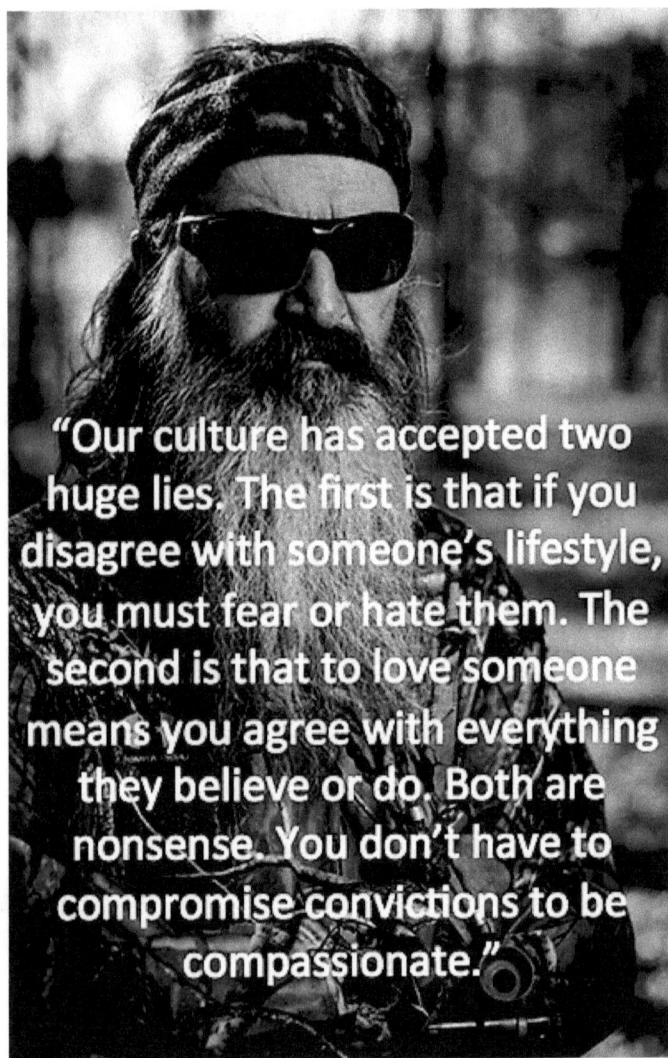

"Our culture has accepted two huge lies. The first is that if you disagree with someone's lifestyle, you must fear or hate them. The second is that to love someone means you agree with everything they believe or do. Both are nonsense. You don't have to compromise convictions to be compassionate."

> **"When you _earnestly_ seek the Lord, He will reveal His Face to you and make known His plans for your life."**

CHAPTER 9

The Most Important Business Relationship That I Almost Lost!

All of this begins with you knowing your identity. And what *you* were created to do.

Once you know that, once I learned these two things, I had perfect clarity and everything else really didn't matter.

Now, every decision I make either lines up with these, or it doesn't. If it doesn't, then it's not a good fit for me and I don't do it... no matter how shiny it looks.

I can now see that all the sparkly opportunities that come my way are not the end game. God has given me the end game for my life, and I would never know that if I hadn't spent an hour per day getting to know Him.

The only way to do that is to spend quiet time with Him every day. That's the sacrifice.

You're giving up other stuff. You're giving up your favorite TV show. Sometimes you're waking up earlier. You're postponing that important thing, your project at work, and you're putting Him first.

I would spend an hour at the chapel every day and sometimes I would lose track of time because I was so deep in conversation with Him that it only felt like we were speaking for 10 minutes.

One time, literally five hours passed by in a flash and I was shocked! I now realize that God is not bound by time or space like we are. He is the Author of Life and time moves according to His will.

As I walked out after 5 hours, my first thought was, *"Man, I just wasted half my day!"* I still had so much work to do, but then I thought, *"Wait a second. I just spent five hours with the Creator of the Universe talking about His plans for my life.*

Honestly, what could possibly be more important than that?"

When I arrived at my office, I completed the entire project in about an hour. Remarkable! It felt almost effortless, like it was nothing.

I felt *super-charged* because I had just been "lit up" by the Creator of the Universe. After that, put any project in front of me and I'm gonna crush it!

That's what happened. It was amazing. If you want everything that God promises, believe Him when He says, *"Put me first, and all these other things I will give to you, all the desires of your heart."*

God knows all the desires of your heart, better than you do. You think you want certain things. You really don't. Those things are actually camouflage for other things that you truly want. That you're not ready to admit, or you don't even know are there deep in your subconscious.

God sees them all.

He will give you all these things, the desires of your heart, but you have to spend time with Him every day.

It's NOT a one-time thing. It's an everyday thing.

God wants a lifelong relationship with you, not a short-term fling. Give God that one hour and He will bless the rest of your day...guaranteed!

Some of the busiest and most productive people on the planet spend one hour a day with God in quiet. If you were to ask them, *"You have one of the most insane schedules on the planet, how do you get it all done?"*

They would probably respond, *"I spend time with God, that's how I do it. He created the entire universe and He knows the future. I don't. He is the absolute best coach I could possibly have. I go and spend an hour with my coach every day before I start my day, and guess what? To the rest of the world, my schedule looks insanely complex but somehow, everything runs smoothly. I make great decisions all day. Most importantly, no matter what's happening around me, I have peace and joy in my heart that the world cannot give."*

PRINCIPLE #11:

It's NOT a one-time thing, it's an everyday thing. God wants a life-long relationship with you. Nothing less will do.

CHAPTER 10

The Best Way To Build A Successful Business Wasn't At All What I Thought!

It's one thing to spend these quiet moments with God, but it's quite another thing to go out and speak about Him in public. That takes guts (well, to be honest, that takes a serious set of balls).

It takes huge courage to do that, especially if like me, you've never done that before. Maybe you've never said the word "God" in the workplace because you fear how people might look at you, or judge you, or maybe opportunities would close because others had a different viewpoint than you.

Duck Dynasty™ is a great example of *marketplace ministry* in action. They're a backwoods family that has stayed true to their values from the beginning.

Fame and fortune hasn't changed them. They don't waiver and they don't apologize for what they believe in. Even when they are publically ridiculed for their Faith, they stand firm.

It sounds warm and fuzzy but does it work?

God continues to bless them for their faith in Him. They bring His message to millions of people just by the way they live. Their actions scream so much more than anything they could ever say.

> *"Preach the Gospel at all times,*
> *and when necessary, use words."*

It was scary the first time I brought God into my business. But I had to try it on and see if it fit. I reminded myself that God owns the past, the present, and the future. He sees what I can't see. All I need to do is take the steps now, and He'll do the rest.

Either I choose to be embarrassed by Him, or I choose to speak boldly, knowing that He'll bless me because of my decision to be faithful.

I don't preach in the workplace. I'm not out asking people, *"Have you been saved?"*

That's not effective. Plus it's not my spiritual gift.

What I do is simple. It's not uncommon at the end of a business meeting for someone to say, *"It was nice meeting you, take care."* I'll often reply with, *"Thanks. Have a blessed day."*

By simply incorporating that little word "blessed" into my regular language, the way I greet people, the way I end conversations, it gets people talking.

Some people smile and tilt their head showing they are pleased by it. Some say, *"A blessed day? I really like that!"* Then others say, *"A blessed day...oh...are you Christian? Me too!"*

That sparks a different conversation altogether. I rarely mention God or say anything about my Faith. But they end up asking questions about me, my faith, or God and it somehow turns into that.

In the past, a few times when that happened and it turned into a God conversation, I would try to shut it down because I thought it was *taboo* to discuss God in the workplace.

But I've grown since then, I've matured.

Now I say to myself, *"Joseph, get out of the way and let God work. Just let it happen."* I simply answer what is being asked by the person and then observe where God will take the conversation.

Once I started doing that, my conversations turned into amazing, intimate connections with people. That possible partnership I thought we were going to lose (because I used the word God) now became a deeper, stronger partnership than ever because I didn't run from who I am.

I'm not telling anyone what to do, but I'm also not running away from who I am and how important God is in my life. And that has changed everything.

Now people know who I am and what I stand for.

For example, I was speaking with gentleman a few months ago when out of nowhere he said, *"Joseph, I think it's really cool how you run your business. It's kind of interesting that you show you're a Christian, and everybody knows you're a Christian. It's not something I would feel comfortable with."*

I remember thinking to myself, *"When do I show I'm a Christian? It's not written on our website. It's not on our business cards, or on any of our marketing material. We're not like, 'Hey, look at us! We're Christians! If you want to work with us, you have to be Christian!'"* No, it's not that at all.

Being Christian is about interacting with people in a very real and human way.

It's about NOT running away from opportunities that present themselves. It's about no longer behaving "bi-polar".

If you're Christian, be a Christian at all times regardless of who's watching or listening. That's the key.

Practicing that has changed everything in my business. Now, opportunities and partnerships come that I wouldn't have ever thought of.

For example, about a year ago God told me in one conversation that I would write a book, and that He would give me the words. I never thought it would happen this soon but here I am writing this book to you. This is not some random accident. I don't believe in accidents, I believe in God. *"Coincidence is merely God choosing to remain anonymous."*

There's no coincidence here. This book is part of His plan for my life.

If nothing else, I hope you take away this:

Your life is a puzzle that only God understands.

Without Him, your future will be locked away from you. You will continue through life, trying to figure it out on your own, spinning in circles.

You'll have small successes, you'll have big failures, but you will never, ever, ever, without God, achieve the greatness that He put within you ----- the greatness that is meant to be shared with the world to make others' lives better.

I feel blessed that He has given me this gift. I feel humbled to give my life back to Him as a gift to be used for His work in the world. This book has nothing to do with me.

My life has nothing to do with me. How many people can say that?

My life has everything to do with Him and others, and that's the point. It's the transformation from self- centered Joseph (with all my empty plans and schemes amounting to nothing), to God-centered Joseph. Now God magnifies my minimal effort so that I have maximum potency in the world.

I can impact other people's lives because it's no longer about me, I stepped aside. I removed myself. I do my best to get out of the way.

But I still fall short many times, there's no question about it. When I step in and try to take control, my life falls apart again. Each time this happens, I just step back out and the pieces come back together.

Is Marketplace Ministry Easy For Me?

Marketplace ministry is the decision to bring God into all areas of my business and to stop being bi-polar (double-sided) with my faith. It means putting Him in charge.

God is the CEO of my company.

On day One, I dedicated the business to Him.

He directs everywhere we go. Whether good things happen or bad things happen, it's totally up to Him.

I just show up every day as "His employee" and answer only to Him. Few people know that about me. Everyone thinks I'm the boss, and that's fine. I am here, at the helm, but He holds the future. He knows all the things that I should and should not be doing for the business.

I'm still learning to go to Him for advice before making any major decisions. It takes a lot of guts, faith and humility to surrender my control because it requires me to surrender my ego, and that's not easy for me.

I am human and like most people, I want to feel loved and accepted. I want to feel validated. I want a pat on the back when I do a good job.

Learning to deflect compliments <u>upwards</u>, knowing that it wouldn't be right for me to take the credit, takes practice.

The first few times I started doing this, it was awkward and uncomfortable. However, as with anything, practice makes it easier. Now it's almost a reflex and I feel great that I'm able to do that for my Creator.

Marketplace Ministry is about completely removing me from the equation. It's about moving my personal and business life from self-centered to God-centered.

It doesn't matter how big our company is. Every day I have to decide how I'm going to behave within our company. How am I going to lead our company?

That doesn't mean I have to push my faith on others. It doesn't mean forcing the people who work for us to believe in the same God I do. That wouldn't work.

It's about stepping back and saying, *"I'm not here to put on a show for anybody. I am here to do right by my Creator. It's between Him and me. That's it. If people are watching and following my example, great—<u>that's between Him and them</u>."*

Our members have different beliefs, faiths, and denominations. I need to respect that. But when I see people doing things that don't align with our core values, then that's a problem I must address.

Our personal core values at the top should literally be our people's core values at the bottom. There should be consistency throughout the entire company.

When I look at really successful brands, one thing most have in common is strong (sometimes polarizing) core values.

Zappos.com is a great example of this.

Not too long ago I met Tony Shei, the founder and CEO of Zappos, while he was giving a talk in Tampa.

He said, *"People are always asking how I made Zappos such a successful brand? Simple, it starts with YOU at the top. It all starts with your personal core values, which means, you must know what you stand for and what you will NOT stand for."*

I have to be black and white to my core. There are no 50 shades of grey. Once I started boldly living my core values, people are watching me and will either be <u>attracted</u> or <u>repelled</u> by how I live.

That's what I want.

The people who are attracted to our values are going to be attracted at a deep level. Those are the people I want to bring on board, or partner with.

The ones who are repelled by our values are the people I don't want to associate with. They tend to cause the most drama and headaches.

I find that strong core values can be a fantastic filtering system for building a quality leadership team of people who will be able to turn our business into a large successful brand.

Indulge me as I clarify a common mistake. Many people have different meanings for the word "brand". Your brand is how you are known in your marketplace to customers, vendors, partners, and mainstream society. You cannot design or 'manufacture' a successful brand. Your brand is who you are authentically, deep down in your core.

It starts with you as the leader of the company, then it's passed down to a few key people who pass it down to even more people.

The outside marketplace observes this and, over time, sees you as either a successful and memorable brand or an absolute failure.

If you're the founder of a large company and have led it a certain way for a long period of time, you may feel it is time for a company transformation.

Maybe God is now tapping on your heart, drawing you towards Him and maybe *Marketplace Ministry* is the way to bring Him into your business.

How do you do that? How do you bring God into your business? Here's the simple answer:

When you transform yourself, He'll transform your business.

Again, the best way to change your business is to start changing yourself. Others will see you and follow you, creating a ripple effect.

Your humble example can change the world. Ghandi was right, *"Be the change you want to see in the world."*

I'm not saying that God will make you a millionaire. That's called "prosperity gospel", and I'm not a fan.

But that doesn't mean you cannot be a billionaire and a good steward of God's wealth like my friend.

He's not greedy with the wealth he's been given because he knows that he's just a "pass-through".

Significant portions of his money go to incredible charitable organizations. He gives his time, energy and resources. I have personally witnessed one of his projects feed over 100,000 hungry children here in the U.S.

He redistributes the financial blessings that have been entrusted to him towards God's work in the world.

Of course, there's nothing wrong with him keeping a small percentage for himself. Even with that small percentage, he's able to live a very nice lifestyle, in a multi-million dollar water-front home with his wife and kids and fancy cars.

He has so much abundance from God passing through his hands because he keeps multiplying his biblical "talents".

To the man who multiplies his talents, more will be given. But to the man who has little and does little, even the little that he has will be taken from him.

Bottom line:

If you're willing to surrender your empty plans and schemes, your self-centeredness and ego, God will do the rest.

You'll wake up with joy in your heart and go to bed with peace on your mind. Every day will be amazing for you.

You'll set down the impossible burden of trying to control your days and smile as God continually brings good people into your life.

While the rest of the world screams, *"Validate me. Accept me. Love me."* ----- you won't have to.

They are searching for what only God can give.

As you start to experience God working in your life, you will step out of the bucket of selfishness and break free from the landmines of temptation.

You will be free.

"The glory of God is a man fully alive in Christ."

PRINCIPLE #12:

Put God first in all areas of your business and personal life and your life will never be the same ----- that is marketplace ministry in a nutshell.

Here's my new mantra
for living a God-centered life:
(feel free to borrow it if you like)

"God first, people second, I am third."

12 PRINCIPLES

FOR LIVING A FEARLESS CHRISTIAN LIFE:

1. Be patient and don't assume you know a person's intentions.

2. *What works in one place, doesn't always work in another.*

3. *Always "mirror" the person you're speaking with. Then add 10% more.*

4. When you are out-numbered, make sure your confidence trumps that of your opponent.

5. *You are NOT defined by what happened in your past.*

6. *When you are looking to partner with someone, speak to their needs FIRST before your own.*

7. *Behind your greatest fear,
   lies your greatest passion and
   until you face it head on and walk
   through its door, you will never
   unleash the greatness that lies within
   you.*

8. *You're never going to be the best in
   the world at your weaknesses.
   Instead focus all of your time, energy,
   and resources on practicing your
   primary strength.*

9. *Until you free yourself and have
   peace about who you are and where
   you come from, you can't fully shine.*

10. *If you are not connected with your
    Creator, you are chasing the wind.
    Most situations are bigger than you,
    that's why you can't control them.*

11. *It's not a one-time thing, it's an
    everyday thing. God wants a life-long
    relationship with you. Nothing less
    will do.*

12. *Put God first in all areas of your
    business and personal life and your
    life will never be the same.*

SUMMARY

When you surrender your life to God, all your problems don't simply fall away. Problems will still come your way. But when you are able to surrender and put Him in charge of the good, the bad, the ugly, and the beautiful... you release the battle for control.

You find peace and calmness within your heart and mind. You reach a point of serenity where, although you will still be faced with personal and business struggles, they will no longer stress you out and steal your energy.

As the storms approach, you'll smile.

You'll see dark clouds and, although you won't know why they're coming, you'll be able to lean back and know they will pass. You'll know that you'll come out on the other side to a bright, sunny day. You'll keep moving forward.

True peace of mind comes from giving everything to God.

At CoCreativ, we're in our first year of business and just getting started. As with any start-up, the first three years are usually a struggle.

But I see the momentum building and things are starting to happen that I couldn't predict.

As I previously mentioned, in prayer the Lord revealed to me that I would write a book and He would give me the words. At first it confused me because I had no idea what He was talking about.

A few months later, Tara Richter, with Richter Publishing, booked a conference room at CoCreativ for her seminar and had a video crew recording testimonials from clients who she had coached to write their own books. One of her clients is a gentleman I know personally: Kevin Harrington (Investor Shark on ABC's Shark Tank).

I thought to myself, *"Who the heck is this girl and how did she get Kevin Harrington (who has an insanely busy schedule) to come in and speak about how great she is at what she does?"* I listened as Kevin and her other clients expressed how quickly she helped them write and publish their books.

I knew I had to speak with her. It was a gut thing. I didn't stop and think, *"Okay, God is sending this person into my life to help me write the book He told me about months ago."* No, that didn't even cross my mind.

I was just so intrigued by her and the people talking about her that I wanted to find out more. While I talked with her she said, *"Okay, I'm going to help you write a book."* I dismissed it but she insisted, *"No, really. This is for real. This is what I do."*

As I'm writing these words, I'm in awe (and still slightly skeptical), that this book will actually get published—because it feels completely surreal.

How is this happening so soon?

But, that's how God works, right? God is our Heavenly Father. He's the Father of all and like any loving father, He loves to give gifts to His children.

God loves to surprise us and surpass our little, pathetic expectations.

When we are ready to receive them, He gives us what He knows are our heart's true desires. And for whatever reason, He thinks I'm ready to publish this book right now.

To be transparent, it's uncomfortable putting my soul out to the world like this. I feel naked. There's more I want to edit, but ready or not, I obey Him.

I hope that the words He's put through my lips inspire you to give your life to Him.

God has a perfect plan for your life that no one else
can do. In all of history, He made only one of you.

**If you are reading this,
YOU are being called right now,
at this very moment,
to spend quiet time with God.**

He is calling because He wants to give you
your Identity, your Destiny and your Assignments.
If you don't feel ready that's okay, I wasn't either.

*"God doesn't call the equipped,
He equips the called."*

Are you ready? God is.

ABOUT THE AUTHOR

Raised by a single mother on welfare, Joseph Warren dreaded their weekly trips to the supermarket and hung his head in shame as they paid for the family's groceries with Food Stamps®.

He made a commitment to himself that when he became a man, his life would be different... he would be happy, healthy and wealthy.

At age 19, Joseph opened a professional fundraising company that specialized in raising funds for non-profit organizations such as The National Center for Missing & Exploited Children (NCMEC).

Within the first 12 months, he grew his startup into a 50-person firm with $2M+ in revenue. Over the next 24 months, he scaled the business into multiple locations (Chicago / Los Angeles / San Diego) and tripled its revenue.

Joseph Warren (along with renowned speaker and author Dr. Alexander Osterwalder and 470 strategy practitioners) co-authored the groundbreaking and best-selling book, "Business Model Generation - A Handbook for Visionaries, Game Changers, and Challengers".

Business Model Generation has become a practical innovation handbook used today by leading consultants and companies worldwide, including IBM, Ericsson, 3M, Intel, MasterCard, Deloitte, NASA and many others.

Find Joseph's Full BIO & Products Here:

www.JosephWarren.net

Joseph M. Warren
Founder and CEO,
CoCreativ Small Business Club™

CoCreativ provides professional workspace and meeting rooms for small businesses from $49/month. No lease, No contract.

You can even have your own private office starting at $299/month. A warm, productive environment with fun, collaborative peeps.

Goodbye Home Office, Hello Office Freedom™

CoCreativ™
WORKSPACE & MEETING ROOMS FOR SMALL BUSINESSES

Questions? Call (727) 277-9522

www.CoCreativ.com

JOSEPH M. WARREN